THE
FIELD & STREAM
Bass Fishing
Handbook

The *Field & Stream* Fishing and Hunting Library

FISHING

The Field & Stream *Baits and Rigs Handbook* by C. Boyd Pfeiffer
The Field & Stream *Bass Fishing Handbook* by Mark Sosin and Bill Dance
The Field & Stream *Fish Finding Handbook* by Leonard M. Wright Jr.
The Field & Stream *Fishing Knots Handbook* by Peter Owen
The Field & Stream *Fly Fishing Handbook* by Leonard M. Wright Jr.
The Field & Stream *Tackle Care and Repair Handbook* by C. Boyd Pfeiffer

FORTHCOMING TITLES

HUNTING

The Field & Stream *Bow Hunting Handbook* by Bob Robb
The Field & Stream *Deer Hunting Handbook* by Jerome B. Robinson
The Field & Stream *Firearms Safety Handbook* by Doug Painter
The Field & Stream *Shooting Sports Handbook* by Thomas McIntyre
The Field & Stream *Turkey Hunting Handbook* by Philip Bourjaily
The Field & Stream *Upland Bird Hunting Handbook* by Bill Tarrant

THE
FIELD&
STREAM
Bass Fishing
Handbook

Mark Sosin & Bill Dance

Illustrated by Dave Whitlock

THE LYONS PRESS

Originally published as *Practical Black Bass Fishing* in 1974 by Crown
Publishers, Inc. The text has been updated and condensed.

First Lyons Press edition—1999

Printed in the United States of America

10 9 8 7 6 5 4 3 2 1

Library of Congress Cataloging-in-Publication Data

Sosin, Mark.
    [Practical black bass fishing]
    The Field & stream bass fishing handbook / Mark Sosin & Bill
Dance ; illustrated by Dave Whitlock.
        p.   cm.—(Field & stream fishing and hunting library)
    Originally published: Practical black bass fishing. New York :
Crown Publishers, 1974. With slight corrections and omissions.
    Includes index.
    ISBN 1-55821-895-5 (pbk.)
    1. Black bass fishing.   I. Field & stream.   II. Dance, Bill.
III. Title.   IV. Title: Field & stream bass fishing handbook.
V. Title: Bass fishing handbook.   VI. Series.
SH681.S67   1999
799.1'77388—dc21   98-45807
                                                                         CIP

Contents

Preface

TOO OFTEN, a book is written and then someone selects a title for it. In this case, we chose the title first, and for good reason. Bass fishing covers such a broad spectrum and is so comprehensive that no single volume or even a series of books can report thoroughly on every phase. Our own experiences have demonstrated that most fishermen thirst for the knowledge and ability to improve their catch, yet they have neither the time nor the inclination to wade through a plethora of literature.

That is precisely why we decided from the beginning to present the *practical* aspects of the subject. By eliminating nonessential material, it became possible to offer a basic yet detailed approach to bass fishing. There are others, to be sure, but we know that this one will work.

Understand from the start that bass offer the supreme angling challenge. They are tough competitors and, at times, they are totally unpredictable. Even the most publicized bass masters are beaten more often than they care to admit, but that's bass fishing—and that is precisely what keeps the millions of bass addicts coming back time after time.

There will be days when no matter what you do, you won't catch bass. And there will be other days when the brightness of good fortune will shine down on the waters you are fishing. Recognize that there is no panacea or cure-all to cover every situation you will encounter when you go bass fishing. The lakes, ponds, and rivers that you fish will have their own peculiarities and idiosyncrasies, forcing you to modify some of the techniques to fit your particular bass holes. However, if you arm yourself with the basics and remain observant, you will extract an extra measure of pleasure in adapting methods to fit your needs.

May we suggest that you study each subject in this book carefully and completely. Keep in mind that you can refer to a specific passage for reference at any time. And if it helps you to catch one more bass than you normally would, we will have accomplished our purpose.

MARK SOSIN
BILL DANCE

Understanding Your Quarry

THE BLACK BASS are probably the most glamorous species in the fresh waters of the world today. They have a high intellect and a strong instinct for survival, but, like all other animals, bass have cycles through their lives that cause them to react in a particular manner. Both the largemouth and the smallmouth approach the physical configuration of the perfect predator, with broad, powerful tails, excellent vision, superb hearing, and the ability to maneuver under water quickly and effectively.

Unlike members of the pike or trout family, the bass is built to probe and forage around logs, rocks, and other forms of protective cover. Sometimes these fish will strike their prey from ambush and other times they'll simply cruise along looking for food. On the other hand, a bass is not tailored to long pursuit, and the chances of a largemouth or smallmouth running down a lure over a considerable distance are slim. Their preferred feeding strategy is to strike instantly when the prey (or lure) passes within range. Burst swimming speed of a bass is about 12 miles per hour, but the sustained swimming speed is much less.

A bass can suspend 2 inches off the bottom or 60 feet off the bottom without expending any more energy. The secret is its swim bladder, an airtight sac that can be inflated or deflated to help maintain a neutral buoyancy. Without it, a bass would sink to the bottom. The swim bladder means that a bass can be at any level, and, as we'll explore in the next chapter, depth is the primary consideration in locating bass.

Being the perfect predator, a bass feeds primarily by sight and sound. Its eyes are well developed, and through a system of orientation to the coming of daylight and darkness, the bass takes full advantage of periods of subdued light. That's one reason bass fishing is often good early in the morning and late in the afternoon. The bass can get closer to its prey and expend less energy in capturing its victim.

As in all fish, the iris in a bass's eye is fixed and cannot open or close down to adjust to the amount of light. This causes the bass to seek shade on a bright day, but there's more to that story. Any predator prefers to remain in darker waters, where it is afforded a certain amount of protection against its enemies while giving it the advantage in the strategy of feeding. It is far easier to see prey swimming by in better-lit water while remaining in semidarkness. And the prey cannot see the bass as well as the bass can see the prey.

Vision, of course, is affected by water clarity. The more turbid the water, the shorter the range of vision and the less time a bass has to decide about striking an offering. Fish know instinctively that once their prey escapes beyond the range of vision, it is gone forever. In clear water, a bass can take more time, but in murky water, it is now or never.

Anglers are always puzzled how a bass can clobber a black lure on a pitch-black night. They can understand the effect of a vibrating lure because they reason that the bass hears it, but something as mundane as a plastic worm raises a question. The answer centers on the lateral line on a bass. This lateral line, which extends from behind the gills to the tail on each side of the fish, is as accurate as radar in pinpointing the presence of an object. It is a hearing organ designed for sounds close to the fish.

Anything moving through the water must displace water molecules. It is precisely this displacement that is picked up by the lateral line, and the fish can strike the source of that sound as effectively as if it were seen with the eyes. The lateral line works only with near-field sounds—those that are within a few feet of the bass—but it is a deadly system. That's how a bass can hit a black plastic worm in deep water on a dark night.

In addition to the lateral line, bass also have ears inside their heads, although they do not have external earflaps as we do. Their bodies act as a sounding board, and they can hear and react to sounds a long distance away. The gentle *plop* of a lure on the water will get their attention, but too loud a disturbance could have the reverse effect, and warning sounds such as a tacklebox scraping on the deck can send a bass scurrying for cover. Sometimes, something as simple as squeaky oarlocks can keep an angler from catching a limit of bass. Simply being aware of what sound can do is half the battle.

COLOR

You bet bass can see color, and even distinguish between various shades. Researchers have concluded that bass see color better than most other fish. The clue to color vision comes from the eye. If a fish has both cone and rod receptors in its eye, you can assume it sees color. The cone receptors are for periods of bright light and mean color vision. The rod receptors are used at night and during periods of low visibility, and basically provide black-and-white vision.

Extensive experiments have been performed on the largemouth to test its color perception. Conclusions point to the fact that the bass sees colors as if it were looking through a pair of yellow glasses. It has difficulty distinguishing yellow from gray, and both yellow and blue are less distinct than other colors. On the other hand, bass see red and violet best and green second best.

Not only can bass discern colors in the water, but they can identify colors and shades in the air before the object touches the water. And their perception is so keen that they can distinguish among 24 different shades.

From an angler's standpoint, bass have been taken on lures of practically every color and shade imaginable. On given days they may show a marked preference for one color. Yet each fisherman has his own favorites, and we certainly suggest experimentation. You have to determine what the fish will strike right now rather than what they hit yesterday.

WATER TEMPERATURE

Fish are cold-blooded creatures and thus their temperatures are governed by those of the surrounding water. Each species exhibits specific temperature preferences, but also has temperature tolerances that cover a much wider range. The largemouth, for example, seems most comfortable when the water is between 65° and 75° F, while the smallmouth likes slightly cooler water (60–70° F). On the other hand, northern anglers often catch largemouths through the ice, which means that the water temperature is between 32° and 39.2° F.

Temperature affects both the occurrence and the well-being of fish, and bass are no exception. As the water chills, their metabolism starts to slow down, and in cold water, bass are very sluggish. They require much less oxygen and food, their digestive rate is very slow, and they don't exert much energy in chasing a lure. If you can find a spot where the water is slightly warmer than the surrounding area (such as the presence of a spring), you can bet there will be a concentration of fish right there.

At the other extreme, bass become uncomfortable when water temperatures rise above 80° F. With higher temperatures, fish require much more oxygen and will usually seek this oxygen above all other considerations. That's when you'll find them along windy shorelines, where a spring enters a lake, or among aquatic plants that produce oxygen.

From an angling standpoint, you must be alert to temperature changes and the response you can expect from bass. Remembering that bass are cold-blooded and take on the temperature of the surrounding water, you can gain some instant intelligence the moment you land a bass. If you have a temperature gauge with you, slip the thermistor into the fish's mouth and down into its stomach. Take a reading. Then lower the thermistor over the side until you find water of the same temperature. That's the depth at which the fish was before you hooked it.

OXYGEN

Without oxygen, fish don't survive. It's as simple as that. To breathe, fish glean dissolved oxygen from the water through their gills. Compared to air, there's so little dissolved oxygen in the water that it is expressed in parts per million. A change of only one part per million can spell the difference between survival and death; it's that critical.

The main source of oxygen in a lake comes from photosynthesis, a process whereby aquatic plants produce oxygen. For that reason, lakes with good vegetation are often rich in oxygen. However, there is another aspect that must be considered: Oxygen is also a vital ingredient in the decomposition of dead plants, phytoplankton, and zooplankton. Too much decomposition and the water becomes oxygen depleted.

There is also an exchange of oxygen between water and air. Flowing water tends to pull oxygen with it, and if the water tumbles over rocks or cascades over a dam or spillway, it picks up oxygen in the process. At times when the oxygen content of a lake is particularly low, look for bass at these oxygen-rich points.

STRATIFICATION

If it weren't for a complete turnover twice a year, most lakes and ponds would become stagnant because of a continued buildup of oxygen-depleted water. As water temperatures drop, water becomes heavier and more dense. Maximum density is reached when the water is 39.2° F. Colder than that, water becomes lighter. That's why ice floats on the surface. If water didn't become less dense as it freezes, the ice would settle to the bottom of northern lakes and destroy all aquatic life.

To trace the cycle: In the fall of each year, water temperatures drop and the heavier water falls to the bottom. This forces the bottom waters to the top, where they once again become reoxygenated; when this happens, the lake is said to "turn over." During this brief period, all levels of the lake have enough oxygen to support life, and bass could be scattered throughout any of the levels.

If the lake is far enough north for the water to reach 39.2° or colder, the 39.2° water will remain on the bottom and ice might coat the lake. The water in the intermediate levels will range between 39.2° and 32°.

In the spring, the process reverses itself. The ice melts, and as the surface waters warm to 39.2°, they become heavier than the water below them and sink to the bottom, once again forcing the bottom water to the top. The sun continues to warm the water and many lakes then become stratified.

On the basis of water temperature, three distinct layers form in a lake. The cold bottom layer is known as the hypolimnion. The warmer surface region is called the epilimnion, and there is a transitional zone between the two called the thermocline. By definition, water temperatures in the thermocline change 0.5° for every foot of depth. The thermocline is a relatively narrow band of water and can be found easily with a thermometer because of this rapid temperature change.

During the summer, the hypolimnion or bottom layer becomes devoid of oxygen, and therefore fish cannot penetrate this zone; that means that all the fish in the lake will be in the upper surface zone (epilimnion) or in the transitional zone (thermocline). Temperature causes this phenomenon, but oxygen is the governing factor concerning the distribution of fish.

FEEDING FACTORS

In order to survive, a fish soon learns to measure the amount of energy it expends in relation to the rewards received. If a bass must expend more energy to catch its prey than the nourishment the prey will bring, it isn't worth the effort. That's why lunker bass often seem extremely lazy, and many knowledgeable anglers counter this trait by working a lure for only a short distance around structure.

When you cast around a stump, you realize that the bass will strike the lure close rather than chase the bait right up to the boat. There are exceptions, of course, but you can waste a lot of time fishing for the exception. A better approach is to fish the structure carefully and then retrieve rapidly for your next cast.

All predators exhibit a number of general tendencies. Two of the most important involve feeding in a school of bait. Contrary to the belief of some fishermen, a bass does not merely open its mouth and swim through baitfish in a random manner. In order to strike, a fish must isolate a specific victim and then pursue it. At the same time, a fish is more prone to select a prey that appears disabled or that looks different from the others.

These principles are particularly significant when bass are feeding on a school of baitfish; they help to explain why bass will strike a lure that lands amid the baitfish and then is retrieved out of the school. The instant the lure clears the school, it is easy for a bass to isolate it and attack; and it looks somewhat different from the other fish in the school.

Bass can be considered general predators and prefer live food or artificials that look alive. Their diet varies, but at times they will specialize for feeding efficiency. As an example, if a lake is loaded with 4-inch shad, the bass may prefer to feed on these, ignoring other foods in the process. In most situations, though, they feed on a variety of baits.

Research has shown that the mature smallmouth bass shows a decided preference for crawfish. For good reason. Smallmouths feeding on crawfish grow much faster than those that don't live where crawfish are abundant. If you're looking for good smallmouth habitat, the first clue is the number of crawfish present. Find crawfish and the smallmouth should be there. You should also recognize that crawfish normally hug the bottom, and smallmouths favoring a crawfish diet would prowl close to the bottom in search of food. To be effective, lures must be fished in this feeding zone.

THE LIFESTYLE OF BASS

Both the largemouth and smallmouth bass spawn in the spring as the water temperature moves from cold to warm. Spawning is triggered by a number of factors and generally takes place when the water is somewhere between 60° and 70° F. At that time, the male bass will move into the shallows and fashion a nest in the bottom. Smallmouths prefer a gravel bottom, while largemouths use either gravel or sand bottoms for nests.

Largemouths nest in about 1 to 3 feet of water within 10 feet of shore, and the nests are spaced at least 20 feet apart as a rule. Smallmouths seem to be more concerned with cover and will build a nest in water ranging from 3 to almost 25 feet in depth. The exact spot is determined by water clarity, and you can assume that the clearer the water, the deeper the nest.

Once the nest is built, the male bass will seek a mate, luring or driving the female over the nest. When she has dropped eggs in the nest, the male will broadcast his milt over the eggs to fertilize them. Each female is capable of producing 2,000–7,000 eggs per pound of body weight, but all the eggs are not spawned at one time. In fact, a male usually spawns with several females, and the same female could spawn with a number of males.

When it's all over, there could be almost 2,000 eggs in a nest. The female then moves into deeper water, and the male remains to guard the nest. It takes between a week and 10 days for the eggs to hatch under normal conditions, but exceptionally warm water temperatures will speed the process. The bass fry are hatched with a yolk sac attached under their gills; the yolk sac supplies food for the first days of life.

A male on guard duty over a nest is particularly aggressive and will strike at anything that comes close to his charges. Bass during this period are very easy to catch if you can find them on the nests, but it also begs the question of how the removal of the male guard (or the female that is about to spawn) will affect the bass population in that particular body of water.

Smallmouths leave the nest before largemouths do, and the tiny fry may be only ½ inch in length when they strike out on their own.

Largemouths may be an inch long when they go it alone. In the process, however, one or both parents might turn on their offspring and attempt to consume them. At times, Papa Bass might devour 80 or even 90 percent of his brood.

Once the yolk sac is absorbed, the baby bass start to feed on live food and will move into the protective cover of the shallows. Until the bass are a couple of inches long, their main diet is composed of tiny crustacea. Then they switch to smaller fish, crawfish, and larger crustacea.

HATCHERY BASS

If you've ever visited a trout hatchery, you were no doubt impressed with the efficiency of technique and the method used to artificially propagate the species. In fact, since trout spawning is directly related to the photo period (amount of daylight), artificial lights can be used to trigger the spawning much sooner than nature gets around to it.

Anglers who have watched biologists "strip" the eggs and milt from trout often harbor the belief that bass can be handled the same way. Bass cannot be "stripped"; they must be allowed to spawn naturally. Perhaps the best explanation of the procedure comes from the Pennsylvania Fish Commission, which tells us that brood stocks of bass must be kept in large ponds. When they build their nests and spawn, biologists must watch the nests closely. After the yolk sac is absorbed, the tiny fry will rise to the surface one time as a group and then settle back into the nest. When this happens, the fish culturist must be waiting with a fine-meshed net to scoop them up. The next time the fry rise from the nest, they disperse and are impossible to catch.

Once the fry are captured, the problems really begin. Unlike trout, which can be fed a diet of commercially available pellets, bass require live food. For the first five weeks—until they reach a length of 2 to 3 inches—the tiny bass are fed a diet of daphnia, a crustacean about the size of a pinhead.

In a hatchery, the young bass must be taught to eat a mixture of finely ground liver and saltwater fish. This is accomplished by mixing the fish meal with the daphnia and then decreasing the amount of daphnia while the fish meal increases. But eventually, the bass want live food again, and they must be fed minnows and crawfish.

You can imagine the problems of obtaining live food. Consider also that it takes much longer to raise bass to stockable size than it does trout, and that Pennsylvania can raise 97,000 pounds of trout per surface acre of raceway in a hatchery; if the same raceways are used for bass, 200 pounds per surface acre is an excellent crop.

For that reason, the few hatchery bass that are produced are earmarked for stocking in new impoundments. Besides, bass in the wild are very prolific spawners.

THE RIDGE LAKE STUDY

In 1941, Dr. George Bennett of the Illinois Natural History Survey began a series of experiments with largemouth bass in an 18-acre impoundment. The impoundment is known as Ridge Lake and the study, which is almost legendary, is still being continued today. A total of 435 largemouth bass (335 of them yearling bass) were stocked in Ridge Lake by Dr. Bennett back in 1941. Three years later, 129 bluegills were stocked.

Fishing was permitted in Ridge Lake on a controlled basis, and a biologist checked the results of each angler. There was no charge for the boats, but all fish caught had to be kept by the angler for the survey. In addition, the water was completely drained out of the lake nine times between 1941 and 1963. Specially constructed weirs were used to capture all the fish in the lake, and the largemouths were kept in special holding pens until the lake refilled. Except for returning the bass that were in the lake at the time of a drawdown, no additional bass were ever stocked.

During the 23rd year of the study, Dr. Bennett calculated that more than 30,000 bass had been removed from Ridge Lake by angling or by scientific culling since the inception of the program. He quickly added that draining censuses confirmed that there were always between 1,500 and 6,000 largemouths in Ridge Lake. All that from the original stocking of 435 fish.

The Confidence Game

BLACK BASS FISHING is changing. At one time, it was strictly a contemplative sport in which the angler silently rowed or paddled along the shoreline, tossing a hunk of wood, plastic, hair, or feathers toward a likely-looking pocket couched in shade or semi-darkness. In some parts of the country, bass fishing still follows this pattern almost exclusively; it's a delightful way to fish *providing* you fully understand that, when you face the shoreline, 90 percent of the fish are behind you in deeper water.

The realization that bass spend a significant portion of their lives away from the shoreline spawned a new breed of bass angler and encouraged the development of new techniques and modified tackle. This recent awareness has often been referred to as the scientific approach, particularly since it encompasses electronic aids such as depthsounders, temperature gauges, oxygen meters, and even instruments to measure the amount of turbidity in the water.

New words entered the vocabulary of every serious bass fisherman. Suddenly there was talk about structure and patterns, and bass fishing in general entered a competitive phase that replaced the contemplative aspects in many sections of the nation. Competition produces benefits. For one thing, it enables an individual to determine how he stands in comparison to other fishermen. And it provides the impetus to learn the latest approaches to bass fishing.

Equally important, competition gives birth to new techniques. There is always someone probing current methods and attempting to come up with a better approach, if for no other reason than to be a better competitor. Competition needs a vehicle where information can be exchanged and results measured. The local bass club was formed to satisfy this need, and it provides the mechanism by which sportsmen can formalize their fishing. At the same time, the formation of the national Bass Anglers Sportsman Society (BASS) did a great deal to help disseminate information on a national scale and even keep the isolated bass angler aware of the latest techniques.

Consider, also, that there is more bass water today in the United States than there was in the days of the pioneers. Most of this water has been created by man through the construction of impoundments and reservoirs. Fortunately, black bass are well suited to the maze of flood-control and water-storage projects that have pockmarked the face of our land. With more habitat and more fish, it is only logical that more people will accept the challenge of our greatest gamefish—the black bass.

THE BEST BASS LURE

Confidence in your ability to locate bass and catch them is by far the greatest lure you have in your tacklebox. You must have complete confidence in what you are doing and the lure you are using. It's a mental attitude, to be sure, but it can make all the difference in the world in catching or not catching fish.

Unfortunately, the majority of bass fishermen pay only lip service to this vital ingredient. Yet if you were given the opportunity to chat with the top tournament bass fishermen, you would quickly realize that every one of them exudes confidence in his approach to the sport. The fact that one man might swear by spinnerbaits while another favors the plastic worm doesn't detract from this confidence. Neither does it matter whether the angler chooses to fish submerged treetops or search for a creek saddle. Each believes honestly that what he is doing will produce bass for him.

To be successful at bass fishing, you have to work at it. There are no miracle methods, no secret lures, and no shortcuts to the thrill of a strike. That's why your attitude must always be positive. You must believe that the next move you make will be the correct one. It's not easy to have confidence all the time, because you can't really fool yourself into thinking you have it. Instead, it is vital that you work at developing the mental attitude that is so important. The ultimate is never to get discouraged and to continue to believe that your approach is the best one for you.

If you fail on a given day, review the procedures you used and the places you fished. Go through a mental exercise and profit from your experience. Tell yourself that next time will be different. Above all, never lose sight of the fact that the reason you love bass fishing is that your quarry is so unpredictable. There will be times when you can't get the lure in the water fast enough and other times when you can't buy a strike regardless of what you do. If bass fishing were routine, you would soon tire of it.

At the end of the day—whether you were successful or not—it's a good idea to check with local guides and marina operators to find out what other anglers did that day. This comparison can add immeasurably to your knowledge. Perhaps you'll learn that no one else caught any fish or that someone mohawked bass on a particular lure or at a specific depth. File the information away in your computer or keep a log and make a note of it. You'll find it could provide the answer on another day when conditions seem similar.

Confidence also extends to the lure you are using. To fish a lure efficiently and effectively, you must first believe in your own mind that the lure you are fishing is the right one. Obviously, if you don't have faith in your lure, your casts are going to be less than accurate and your retrieves mechanical. Chances are that you'll change lures quickly and continue to change.

You gain confidence through experience and understanding. It starts with a comprehension of the habits and habitat of your quarry, which in turn dictates how and where you should fish and the tackle you should use. This book has been tailored to help you learn more about bass fishing and to instill in you the confidence that is so crucial. In many instances you'll discover that your approach is the preferred one, and we hope there will be other suggestions that will lead you to explore bass hideouts and techniques that you haven't tried before.

CASTING ACCURACY

Every competent bass fisherman we've ever had the pleasure of meeting and observing on the water proved to be an extremely accurate caster. He could place a lure exactly where he wanted it time after time. And he exhibited superb familiarity with the tackle he was using, whether it was spinning or bait-casting gear, or a fly rod.

You'll discover that the ability to drop a bait on a precise spot will mean more fish on a consistent basis. Nothing destroys confidence faster than the frustrating tendency to hang a lure in the bushes or let it fall in a brush pile instead of alongside the brush. By the time you retrieve your lure, you might as well look for another spot.

Casting is a learned routine, and anyone can perfect his accuracy. All it takes is practice and more practice. The best time to improve your accuracy is when you are on dry land. If you wait until you're fishing, you'll end up wasting precious time. Simply set aside a few minutes each day and practice in the backyard or at a nearby park. Always select a target whenever you cast and try to put the lure on the mark.

HOW LONG SHOULD YOU FISH EACH SPOT?

Beginning bass fishermen seem to be plagued by the question of how long they should work each location. In time, the answer becomes very apparent, but since the question does harbor importance for many anglers, let's tackle it right away. Again, confidence is the key. The moment you have lost confidence in the location, it's time to move on—or at least try to regain the confidence. Otherwise, you'll be going through the motions, but you won't have the concentration and thought behind your technique.

Normally, you should fish a spot until you have worked it thoroughly at all depths with an assortment of good lures in several colors, using variations in your retrieve. That might mean a few casts or it could dictate a couple of hours. Remember that even the correct lure fished at an incorrect depth or with the wrong retrieve might mean that you are doing nothing more than enjoying the great outdoors.

We're not trying to sidestep this question, but are simply pointing out the many variables in the answer. As an example, if you fish a particular spot regularly, you soon gain a feel for exactly where the fish should be, the lure to use, the type of retrieve, and even the direction of the retrieve. In that type of situation, you would probably have a pretty good idea whether fish were there or not on a given day. You wouldn't be probing, because experience has given you a great deal of information about that single spot. Under those circumstances, a spray of fan casts could tell the story.

Picture yourself, however, on an unfamiliar lake working a similar location. You have some thoughts on where the fish should be, but you'll have to work longer to determine if they are there or not. And you must also consider the degree of confidence and experience you have acquired. The veteran angler can cover an area somewhat more quickly than the neophyte and know that he has done the job thoroughly.

BEING OBSERVANT

Your degree of alertness and powers of observation are excellent indicators of the amount of concentration and confidence you have at the moment. If you persist in worrying about what happened at the office, at home, or somewhere else, you might as well put the boat back on the trailer and pick another day to fish. Bass fishing requires complete concentration.

When we discuss the establishment of a pattern, you'll see how important observation can be; but even in general bass fishing the ability to know what is taking place around you can tip the scales toward success. Bass fishing is often opportunity fishing. You must recognize a set of circumstances and then take advantage of them.

A good angler hears as well as sees, and his mind registers the impressions. If, for example, a bass slaps a baitfish on the surface behind you, your ears should convey the message, even though you are concentrating on casting to a target. The trick is to train your senses to accept the commonplace in nature and seek out the unusual. Let's carry the question of sound a step farther. Perhaps shad are frolicking on the surface. Your ears register and accept this sound as normal. But a deeper splash that signals a predator feeding on a minnow should attract immediate attention.

Top-ranking bass fishermen are forever able to recall the circumstances surrounding the catching of bass after bass. They seem to remember water depth, type of lure, speed of retrieve, and a host of other variables. They have total recall of these facts even years later. If we can interpret this uncanny ability, it boils down to concentration and observation. Nothing they do is haphazard. Each piece of the puzzle fits into place in their minds. When you train yourself to concentrate as thoroughly as they do, you're well on your way to becoming a top bass angler.

CHAPTER 3

Establishing a Pattern

BASS, LIKE ALL other animals, are creatures of habit and exhibit a lifestyle tailored to optimize food, protection, and comfort. The name of the game is survival and both the largemouth and the smallmouth play it well. Although there are exceptions to every generality, for purposes of discussion we can conclude that the majority of the bass in a given lake will be doing relatively the same thing at the same time.

Pattern is a word used to describe what a proportion of the bass are doing at a specific instant in time or what stimulus these fish might respond to. We can also define pattern as the type of place beneath the surface that a great many bass are using at the same time. To fully understand the concept, you must recognize that there could be several patterns in effect at the same time. Not all bass will be following the same one, but for you to be effective, you need only uncover a single pattern.

A pattern is often dictated by food supply, oxygen content, water temperature, time of day, and even time of year. The key to successful bass fishing is the ability to locate a pattern quickly and then stick to it until it fails to produce fish. Patterns take many forms and can even be said to include the type of lure and the speed of retrieve.

Let's concentrate most of our efforts on the *type* and *depth* patterns.

TYPE PATTERN

The need to be alert and observant is the single key to finding pattern. The typical fisherman is so busy fishing that he often overlooks the signs of a pattern. He may be on the best pattern the lake has to offer, yet fail to recognize it as such. Top bass fishermen will amaze you with their ability to tell exactly what they did when they hooked a bass. They have an idea of the type of terrain, speed of retrieve, depth position of the lure, and a host of other factors. This ability is learned and developed, and we suggest that you work at honing your own powers of observation toward this goal.

Let's assume the average fisherman is casting a shoreline and suddenly hooks a bass. He continues working the shoreline and a little farther down hooks another bass. The tendency is simply to assume that he happened on a spot or two that held a bass. What he may very well have overlooked was that his first 50 casts were made at the bases of cypress trees and the 51st cast, which took the bass, happened to land alongside a willow tree. If the angler noted this mentally, then he would have become excited when the second bass struck, because that was also at the base of a willow tree.

Knowing this, our angler could then concentrate his energies on skimming the shoreline and looking for willow trees. There is every indication that a willow tree in the same depth of water would hold a bass.

We had a similar experience one day while fishing Sam Rayburn Reservoir in eastern Texas. The fish were in 17 to 20 feet of water, and every time we spotted an ironwood bush and the depth was right you could bet your rod and reel that a fish would hit. That's pattern fishing.

The more you fish a particular lake, the more you know about it and the easier it is to find a pattern. You also have the advantage of knowing similar spots the moment you do find a pattern. The reason for searching for a pattern is that fishing time is short; to maximize the utilization of the limited time all of us have, it makes sense to catch fish, and finding the pattern is the easiest way.

In searching for a type pattern, you must be alert to types of bottom. A bank may run from mud to rock to gravel. You catch a bass at the spot where rock turns to gravel; you continue moving down the bank and it happens again where rock turns to gravel. That's your pattern, and you immediately concentrate on those spots where rock turns to gravel. Bypass the other types of shoreline and jump from place to place that meets these conditions.

DEPTH PATTERN

You can almost determine the skill of a bass fisherman by the second question he asks you. If you pass someone on a lake, he might ask how fishing is. You reply by showing him a couple of lunkers or by telling him you managed to fool a couple of bass. The most important question he can ask you is to tell him the depth at which you caught your fish.

Beginners have a tendency to begin a line of questioning about what lure you were using, how fast you worked it, or even where you caught the fish. But a knowledgeable bass master need only know the depth at which the fish were taken and he can put every piece of the puzzle together.

The single most important factor in bass fishing is finding the right depth. If you are not fishing the right depth, you're wasting your time. The best fisherman can fish the best lure in the world, but if he's fishing the wrong depth, he won't catch fish. At the right depth, almost anyone can catch fish.

We were fishing a lake in Florida that has any type of vegetation you could ask for. After spending a great deal of time fishing various places without enjoying a single strike, we pulled into a spot that had a small patch of lily pads about 20 feet square. After tossing a worm, spoon, and spinnerbait without a hit, we were about to seek greener pastures when we noticed three small lily pads isolated from the others. Each pad was about 6 inches in diameter. Easing over with the electric motor, we made a cast, let the worm sink into the grass, and started the retrieve. As the worm passed the clump of three lily pads, a bass picked up the worm and we set the hook. It wasn't a big bass, but on a fishless day, anything is greatly appreciated.

After landing that bass, a few more casts proved that it was a lone fish, so we eased over to the pads and found that the water was 2½ to 3 feet deep. Visions of a pattern raced through our heads as we began to search for isolated clumps of lily pads. The next bunch of pads didn't produce fish, and when we measured the water depth we found it was 1½ to 2 feet. We then edged the boat into slightly deeper water and discovered that when we found a few lily pads in 3 feet of water, we took a bass. If the pads were in 2 feet of water, they would be fishless. These weren't trophy bass, but they did provide plenty of action.

FINDING THE RIGHT DEPTH

The better you know a lake, the easier it is to determine the correct depth on a given day. You already know a number of spots, and chances are that at least one of them will produce a fish or two, thus giving you depth information. There really isn't an easy way to find the right depth, but there are a few tips that might shorten the time.

Before you crank the engine on your boat, you should have been talking to the boat dock operator, any of the local fishing guides around, and even anglers who have just come back to the dock. Remember that right after you ask them how the fishing has been, inquire about the depth. They can give you some vital information.

Depth, of course, is directly related to temperature, and bass have a preferred comfort zone even though they are not always within that zone. Experience has shown that bass often hang out near the bottom in temperatures between 65° F and 75° F. It's easy enough to run the boat into deep water, drop a thermometer over the side, and read the depths at which this temperature range occurs. Then look for bottom structure within that preferred depth zone. Work different areas within that depth until you catch a fish. Note the depth and the type of place, so you can begin to establish a pattern.

We cannot overemphasize the importance of being observant. If you have difficulty in remembering, a notebook will solve that problem. Write it down and then keep the information in your tacklebox so you can refer to it constantly.

Long, Sloping Points

Veteran bass anglers have discovered that if they must find the pattern depth quickly, long, sloping points extending out into the lake are the answer. They can work from the shallow beginning of the point, moving deeper and deeper until they find a fish. Usually, the better points for this type of exploring taper gradually rather than drop off abruptly.

To be productive, these points should have deep water on both sides, and if a submerged creek channel swings close by, so much the better. A narrow point extending into the lake is better than a very wide point, because you can cover it in fewer casts and the fish will be more concentrated if they are somewhere along that point.

Bass, and especially lunkers, demand plenty of deep water nearby. A point that meets this requirement should be a feeding station, and if bass are on it, you should find them. A creek channel adds spice to the terrain, but it is not really necessary (see illustration 1 on page 20). Work the point carefully, fanning your casts until you cover both sides. Then move down about a half cast and repeat the procedure.

Most of these points are really part of the secondary bank of the lake and may slope on one side and drop off abruptly on the other (see illustration 2). If these underwater points have brush or other cover close by, they will be even better.

During the spring and fall, one of the best places for big bass on a lake at home looks like illustration 3. Ninety percent of the time, the bass are taken along the three points with deep water on both sides. They are actually tiny peninsulas extending into the deeper water. Without a depthsounder, you would be hard pressed to locate these points.

In the spring, as water temperatures begin to warm, most of the fish hug the upper point where the water drops from 12 to 20 feet. During the fall, the other two points are usually more productive.

CASTING A POINT

The normal tendency when fishing a point is to start shallow and continue working into deeper and deeper water. This method is generally productive, but you should be aware of other ways to fish the same area. Instead of starting along the shallow base of the point and fishing deeper, you may want to start in deep water and make your casts into shallower and shallower water.

It goes without saying that if you want to keep your lure along the bottom, it is much easier to fish from the shallows to the deep. But fish won't always hit a lure in that direction. That's why you want to vary your approach. If you don't take a fish from shallow to deep, reverse the procedure and fish from deep to shallow.

A third way of fishing the same area is to keep the boat parallel to the drop-off and use a series of fan casts to move the lure right along the drop-off. By paralleling, you can work the lure up the slope for a short distance or drag it down the slope, depending on your angle of cast.

The important consideration is the realization that lure direction is another variable that should be considered in determining pattern. On some days the fish will clobber a bait from shallow to deep and other days from deep to shallow. Try all approaches before you convince yourself that it's time to move to another point.

THE COUNTDOWN METHOD

It's one thing to be over the right depth of water and quite another to have your lure at the right depth. If you were to talk to a top-rated bass angler right after he made a cast, chances are that he wouldn't hear you or at least wouldn't take the time to give you an answer. The reason is that he's too busy counting.

Unless you are using a lure that floats on the surface, the trick is

I. An ideal secondary point

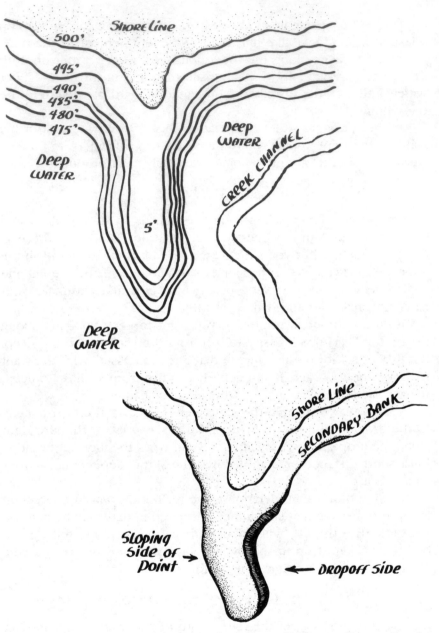

Shore Line

500'
495'
490'
485'
480'
475'

Deep
WATER

Creek Channel

Deep
Water

5'

Deep
WATER

Shore Line

Secondary Bank

Sloping
Side of
Point →

← Dropoff Side

2. A long, sloping underwater point

to count as the lure sinks so that you have a reference point for depth. Each angler has his own counting method, which could be a rhythm such as "1 a-n-d 2 a-n-d 3 . . ." or "1,000 and 1, 1,000 and 2,

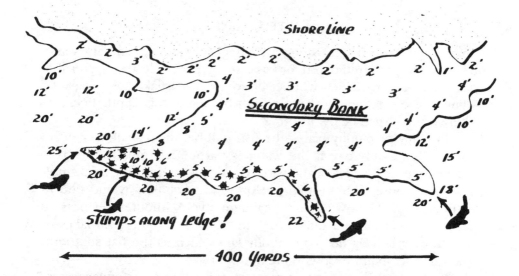

1,000 and 3 . . ." What you say to yourself is unimportant as long as you can approximate seconds of time.

The countdown method lets you know the depth of your lure at a given instant in time. You cannot fish scientifically without using the countdown method—it's that important. As an example, you could be working a sloping point and would have no way of knowing where your lure was unless you counted. Your cast may have been a shade too far and you could have dropped the lure over the edge of the drop-off. By counting down, you can tell this instantly. Perhaps there's a sudden drop-off that you didn't know existed. The countdown method will tell you that your lure is still falling even though it should have hit bottom. The corollary is also vital. A lure that stops too soon might have hit a ledge, but a better alternative is that a bass grabbed it as the lure was falling.

It's all part of the total picture you must maintain at all times. You must be mentally oriented by remembering the configuration shown on a contour map and orienting it through a depthsounder to the water below you. As the boat drifts or turns, the countdown method will tell you if you are casting the area you should be. After all, it looks so nice and neat in diagrams or on a topo map, but on the water you just don't have the reference points.

Above all, the countdown method helps you to concentrate and keeps you alert. Instead of permitting your mind to wander and perhaps miss an important concept, it forces you to count and think about what you are doing.

WATER CLARITY

Even before you begin fishing a particular lake, you can gain some clues about preferred depth for bass. As a general rule, the clearer the lake, the deeper the fish will be. Of course, if the lake has a thermocline in the summer, the fish will not be below this depth, because there is no oxygen below it.

In dingy or muddy water, the fish will be much shallower, even on a bright sunny day. If the water is particularly muddy, the bass may be within 15 feet of the surface, since a muddy lake might not have any appreciable visibility below that level. Bass would find it difficult to feed below this minimal light level. Without cover, bass in lakes such as Ouachita, Bull Shoals, and Table Rock—all clear lakes— would be relatively deep. In muddy lakes such as the flat southern lakes, 15 feet might be a working bottom limit.

If you can see a white lure down to a depth of 3 feet under water, the bass in that lake are probably no deeper than 15 feet. But if you can see a white lure down to 12 feet, the bass could be as deep as 30 feet or more.

THE DEEP, CLEAR LAKE MYSTIQUE

Even some of the best bass fishermen go to pieces if they are forced to fish a deep, clear lake. Thermoclines and other fishing limitations to the contrary, these anglers are overwhelmed by the mere thought that a lake might be 200 feet deep out in the center and plummet to 60 or 80 feet near some shorelines. They have visions of fish being at any depth and roaming all over the lake vertically and horizontally.

If you are faced with this situation, think through the problem. You'll soon realize that most of the fish in the deep lake will be between the surface and 35 feet or perhaps 40 feet. It's really no different than fishing a lake that is only 40 feet deep. Of course, because the lake is clear you could assume that the fish would be a little deeper than if they were in dingy water, but you're not going to fish very effectively below 40 feet, so concentrate between 15 and 35 feet and you should find all the fish you need.

Should a deep lake still prove troublesome, try to relate to a favorite lake back home. Scout the terrain until you find something that resembles a home-lake hot spot. Then start fishing it. Chances are you'll begin to catch fish.

CONTOUR MAPS

Contour or topographic maps have become as useful to the modern bass fisherman as treasure maps were to the pirates of the 18th century. Without these magical guides, locating pay dirt can be a difficult task.

Recognize, however, that *not all* topographic maps contain depth information, and this is particularly true of natural lakes. If you plan to fish a man-made impoundment, the oldest map available might be the best one because it shows the area before it was flooded. Sometimes the newest map will do the job for you. The point to remember is that there are differences in topographic maps, and not all of them have the necessary contour information for fishermen.

When you receive your topographic map of the area you want to fish, you may discover that the reservoir or impoundment is not shown. The map may have been drafted before the reservoir was built, and this is precisely what makes it so valuable. Your first job is to outline the reservoir. Anyone who has fished impoundments knows that the water level varies with the season of the year and the amount of rain in the area or throughout the drainage basin. Water level is known as pool stage or pool elevation, and it can also be adjusted by opening or closing the floodgates on the dam.

Your initial interest is in normal pool elevation—the amount of water the reservoir was designed to hold. This is always expressed in feet above sea level. It is usually noted on the topographic map, but you can either ask the Geological Survey to note it for you or check with the Corps of Engineers for the information.

A contour map is a maze of lines connecting areas of the same elevation. There are different-scale maps, and the one you want is the map with the smallest intervals between contour lines. Standard intervals are 5 feet, 10 feet, and 20 feet of elevation. Five-foot intervals show much more detail for the fisherman than 10- or 20-foot intervals.

For purposes of illustration, let's assume that the normal pool elevation is 500 feet above sea level. Take a felt-tip marker and trace the 500-foot elevation lines wherever they appear on the map. This will be the normal shoreline of the impoundment. A transparent marker can then be used to color in the area of the impoundment.

If you are using a map with 5-foot intervals, you know that each succeeding line inside the reservoir represents 5 feet of depth (see illustration 4 on page 26). By subtracting the elevation shown on a

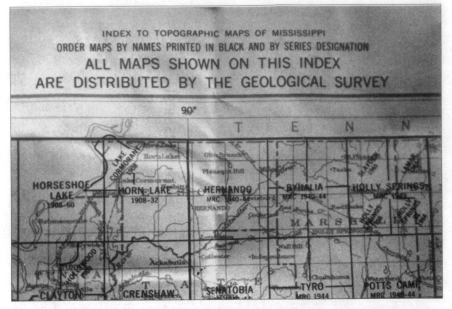

To order topographic maps you must first obtain an index and then request maps by name and series designated. If you are not certain which maps to order, write for a free index to: USGS Information Center, Box 25286, Denver, CO 80225.

specific contour line from the pool elevation of 500 feet (in this case), you can also arrive at the depth of any area.

Since most bass fishing is done from the shoreline to depths of 35 or 40 feet, you can see the need for 5-foot intervals on a map. When these interval lines are very close together, you can tell at a glance that there is a rapid drop-off. The tighter the lines, the sharper the drop-off.

To compensate for winter and spring rains, some lakes are drawn down from a high pool to a low pool. Pool elevation may be 500 feet in June and only 480 feet in September. In determining depth, you simply subtract elevations from the new pool stage. Most local newspapers provide daily lake readings so that you know the exact pool stage.

Underwater real estate is seldom flat and level. Usually, there are humps and rises that reach toward the surface, and many of these are good places to fish, especially when there is deep water nearby. The current depth of any rise in the bottom can be determined by subtracting that elevation from the height of the pool stage (see illustration 5); and the closeness of interval lines will tell you if it slopes upward or rises sharply.

TRIANGULATION

Once you begin studying your contour map, you'll quickly become convinced that it can be the best fishing partner you ever had. Recognize that it will take practice to read it effectively and that you will need a little experience to relate the map to the actual physical terrain. Everything on a map can appear neat and clean, yet when you're on the water, you have to orient the map to the landscape and your depthsounder.

The technique of triangulation will help you to locate spots that are out in the middle of the lake and not on the shoreline. Remember that 90 percent of the fish are usually in deeper water around some type of underwater structure. Your job is to find these places, and once you do, you want to be able to return to them easily. That's where triangulation comes in.

You can triangulate without the use of any sighting devices, but it is often much easier if you carry a small sighting compass with you. These are available at most outdoor stores and fit neatly in your tacklebox. You should always carry a compass on the water anyway, in addition to the one on your boat, and a sighting compass will serve both purposes.

If you use a sighting compass to triangulate, position the boat over the spot and select a prominent object on shore. It could be a tree, a house, a notch in a bluff, or any one of a thousand things. Chances are it appears on your contour map. If it doesn't, mark it in. Use your sighting compass to take the compass bearing of this object. In nautical terms, this gives you a line of bearing. Let's assume you picked a smokestack that was due east or 090° on the compass.

Now you must select a second object at approximately right angles to the first. You pick a water tower that is almost due south or 178°. Mark the object and its bearing on the chart. To find this exact spot again, you run on one of the lines of bearing. That is, you would start with the smokestack bearing 090° (due east) and run directly toward it on this bearing. Keep checking the cross bearing until the water tower is exactly 178°. You are now directly over the spot.

In selecting objects, make sure that they will look the same at all seasons of the year. Too often, an angler will select a tree that has unique foliage and then discover that in the late fall when the leaves are on the ground, he can't find his marker. (Speaking of markers, if you leave a buoy over the spot it might get moved or serve as an invitation to others to concentrate on this spot.)

4. Pool elevation

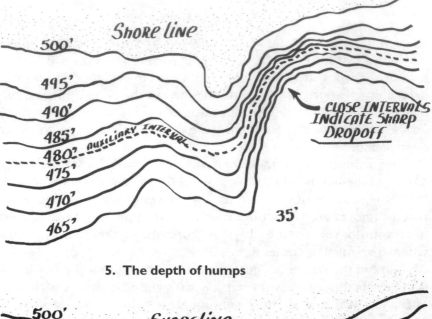

5. The depth of humps

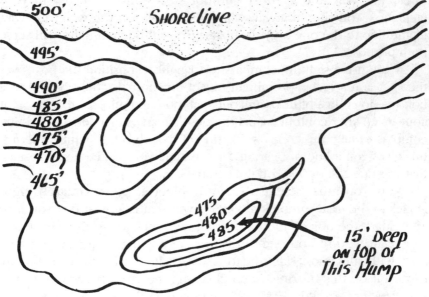

If there are enough prominent features around a lake or features that you can distinguish easily, you can use another method of triangulation. Instead of a compass, you can use a range to locate a line of bearing. A *range* is the nautical term to describe two objects on shore in direct line with each other. If you were to select a prominent tree

6. Triangulation

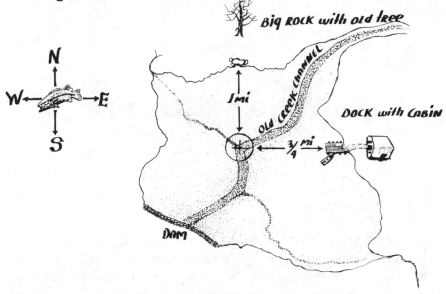

on the shoreline and line this up with a shoreline rock in front of the tree, you would create a range. Establish a second range at approximately right angles to the first—a dock with a cabin, for example—and you have triangulated your fishing spot.

To return to the spot, you simply run one of the ranges and keep checking until the second range forms. As an example, line up the rock with the prominent tree and run directly toward it. When the other two objects you have selected at right angles are in line, you're over the spot you want to fish.

In the course of time, you'll locate a multitude of places in a particular lake and you'll soon start to forget some of them unless you use a system for remembering. The best system we have found is to give each spot a name. Select a name that is seemingly ridiculous, but easy to remember. You might call it Lunker Haven, Honey Hole, Animal Farm, Jewelry Store, or any other name that comes to mind. You can also record the name in your notebook. It will probably come in handy when you're trying to figure out where to fish next someday in the future.

Locating Structure

I T IS IMPOSSIBLE to tell when the first bass fisherman turned his back on the shoreline and decided that most bass spend the major part of their adult lives in deeper water. Possibly the early beginnings of fishing for bass in deeper water happened more by accident than by design.

Structure fishing is the modern bass angler's cornerstone of success. With the ability to locate structure comes a working knowledge of the black bass, its habits, and its habitat. Consider that many of the large reservoirs across our country offer hundreds of miles of shoreline and thousands of acres of open water. That's a lot different from the tiny farm pond or tank out behind the barn where you can cast the shoreline a couple of times each evening, covering every foot of it.

If you're going to find fish on big water, you have to know where they are most likely to appear and then concentrate your efforts on only those spots that offer the greatest promise. You won't be right every time you launch your boat, but the law of averages is tipped heavily in your favor.

WHAT IS STRUCTURE?

Consider structure to be the floor of the lake extending from the shallows to the deeper water. More precisely, it is unusual or irregular features on the lake bottom that are different from the surrounding bottom areas. A stump tipped on its side in a foot or two of water along the shoreline would be structure, and a creek bed meandering along the bottom of the lake at a depth of 25 feet is also structure.

Structure comes in all sizes and shapes. It can be straight or crooked, contain dents and depressions, or be flat. Some structure is long while other is short. Some is steep, sloping, barren, brushy, grassy, stumpy, rocky, mossy, or stepped. It can be shallow or deep— on the shoreline or offshore in open water.

One of the best ways to grasp the concept of structure is to use your imagination when you're driving along a highway. Look at the surrounding countryside and picture what it would look like if the entire area were suddenly inundated with water. Start trying to pick the places where bass would be most likely to hang out. You might start with the drainage ditch alongside the road you're driving on and around the culvert you just crossed.

As you go through these mental gyrations, you will start to associate stands of trees along the field perimeters as a specific type of structure. Some fields will slope and others will be flat, perhaps with a drop-off on one side. The idea is to be able to visualize what your favorite lake might look like if the water were suddenly drawn down. Most anglers find it difficult to picture the physical features of a lake bottom once it is covered with water. You know that there's a roadbed or ditch down below the surface, but unless you train yourself, you don't always visualize it when you are fishing.

A map and depthsounder can help you to gain the necessary mental picture, but if you also associate features with those you can see above the ground, it becomes a lot easier. Then, the next time you fish a creek bed shouldering into a point, you might be able to compare it with one you've seen on the way to the lake.

THE GOLDEN RULE

For any type of structure to be productive, it must have immediate access to deeper water. This rule applies regardless of whether the structure sticks up out of 3 feet of water near the shoreline or happens to be a stand of trees in 35 feet of water in the center of the lake.

Bass consider the quick passage to deep water an escape route from predators or any type of danger. Call it instinct or habit, but bass won't wander very far from that escape route. Like submarines, the bass want the option of crash diving when they feel it necessary.

The same largemouths and smallmouths need a route to travel from their home in deep water to shallower areas for feeding. We believe that creek or river channels moving under a lake are in reality highways for bass, and that bass move up and down the creek channels just as a car moves along a road. There are other routes, to be sure, but creek channels are one of the best.

Another theory says that bass don't simply swim from deep water to shallow water without pausing along the way. Usually the fish will hesitate at natural breaks, which might be the edge of the drop-off or some kind of object at that junction. Some anglers believe that they may rest in these areas for periods of from a few minutes to a few hours. At any rate, keep in mind that not all bass move into the shallows at the same time, so there are always some fish along the deeper structure.

A Buoy System

Someone once said that a picture is worth a thousand words, but when you're trying to imagine what underwater structure looks like, a picture may be worth ten thousand words. The only way to capture the picture is to drop marker buoys in a pattern designed to trace out the structure. It's going to take a little time to do it right and it may require a dozen marker buoys or more, but it also could lead to the largest stringer of bass you've ever taken.

We believe it is worth the extra effort to catch fish. When you have planned and plotted your search for bass and are successful, it is the greatest feeling in the world. There's nothing comparable with finding something you cannot see.

It almost goes without saying that you must carry a good supply of buoys aboard your boat. We prefer to carry ours in two distinct colors so that we can mark either side of a channel or deep and shallow water. You can fashion your own buoys in a variety of ways. A piece of Styrofoam with some line wrapped around it and a weight works fine. Buoys are also available commercially and can be purchased individually or in kits of a half dozen or more.

Dropping buoys is pretty much a matter of common sense. Your goal is to outline the structure so that you can find the exact location of a drop-off or follow a curve or bend in a creek channel. In buoying a drop-off (illustration 7), you must work the boat back and forth, using your depthsounder to select each point where water depth begins to drop. Note that we would start in one corner and follow an in-and-out path (dotted line), tracing the entire point. If you find that one area has a particularly sharp drop-off or some irregular feature, you can use a different-colored buoy to mark it.

Once you have finished dropping the buoys, the underwater picture begins to come into focus. The best approach is to take out your

7. Buoying a drop-off

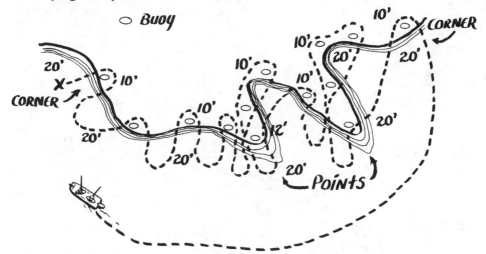

8. Dropping buoys along a creek channel

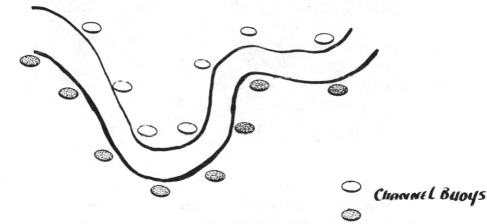

notebook and sketch the outline of the structure, using reference points where possible to orient it.

After you have recorded your find, you're ready to fish it, and you'll discover that the buoy system will guide each cast and help you to cover the area thoroughly. When you have fished the spot completely, ease through it again and retrieve your buoys.

When you are marking a creek channel, use two separate colors to denote each side of the creek, and follow the bends in the creek carefully. If you drop buoys at closer intervals, you'll trace a better outline. As you become more experienced, you won't need as many buoys to tell you how the creek meanders (illustration 8).

9. Marking a ridge

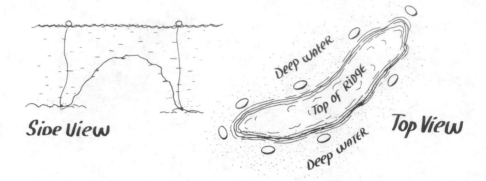

10. Marking a hump

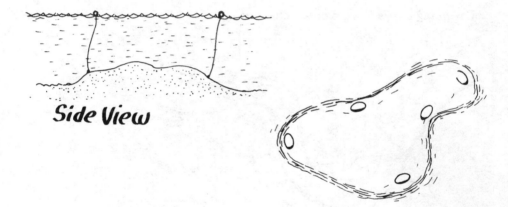

An underwater ridge can be fished by sitting over deeper water and casting into it or by sitting over the ridge and working your lure from deep to shallow. A third option is to sit off one of the points and cast parallel to it. No matter how you plan to fish it, your buoys should mark both ends of the ridge and both sides (illustration 9).

A hump or sheepback should be buoyed on all sides (illustration 10), and the number of buoys again depends on the area involved. Don't skimp when you drop buoys. It's better to use an extra one or two than to become confused on the structure shape. The side of the hump closest to deeper water will be the best, and you might want to mark this with buoys of a different color.

Don't fall into the trap of laziness. It's easy to convince yourself that you don't have to mark out a new spot before fishing it, but you must also accept the risk of not fishing it properly.

CREEK BED POINTS

If you were to limit an experienced structure fisherman to one type of underwater terrain, his first choice would undoubtedly be a creek channel. Channels wind their way across and around the lake floor in every man-made reservoir or impoundment, and they are present in a number of natural lakes. As we mentioned earlier, bass use these creek channels as highways, and there are times when they will use the channels for shade and cover.

Anytime a creek channel runs in close to the bank or a point, it has to be a good place for bass. You may not always find the bass in residence, but sooner or later they should be there. These creek bed points, however, are always worthy of your attention, and if you're going to fish points, pick the ones where a creek is nearby.

In illustration 11 (see page 34), we show a typical shoreline that might occur in any type of lake—lowland, midland, or highland. This classification is primarily based on elevation, and each type of lake exhibits certain typical characteristics. Highland lakes are in hilly country and are usually deep and clear. Lowland lakes are shallow, flat lakes at low elevations that have a minimum of structure because the surrounding terrain is relatively flat. Midland lakes are found at intermediate elevations and exhibit characteristics of the other two.

All three points in the illustration (#1, #2, and #3) look as if they would hold fish, and they very well might, but Point #2 would obviously be the most productive. The reason is that #2 is a creek bed point—that is, the creek coming out of the cove moves right alongside this point of land.

Throughout this book we will continually try to make you aware of the fact that you have only a limited amount of time to fish, and that time should be spent on places offering the greatest potential. We'll suggest you pass up other places that might look good in favor of those that experience demonstrates to be the best. Here is a typical example:

The creek bed point is an excellent place to find and catch bass. Let's assume you have located a school of largemouths at daybreak one morning on the inside cove end of Point #2 (marked Spot A). It's a great beginning and you pick up a few fish, or perhaps you take your limit right there.

The next morning you can't wait for the alarm clock to ring; you rush through breakfast and hurry right back to Spot A. You're using the same lure and technique you employed yesterday, but this morn-

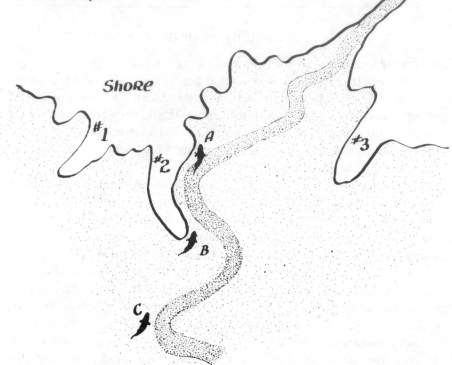

Shore

#1

#2

A

B

C

ing you draw a blank. That's when you start analyzing the situation. There could be several reasons, and it's your job to find the right one.

Your first two impressions would be that the fish either have moved or for some unknown reason aren't hitting. These mental exercises may pacify the mind, but they are not going to catch fish for you until you begin to experiment. The bass may not prefer yesterday's lure, so you had better get busy trying a variety of other offerings. Possibly it's the retrieve that is bothering them. Yesterday they wanted the lure slow, but today they want it fast or they want it with a stop-and-start motion. Maybe they are a little deeper than yesterday, so you try that, too.

When you have gone through the routine and still haven't produced results, you must assume that the fish aren't there. That's a far better option than throwing in the sponge and convincing yourself that they are there but won't hit. This is where a good contour map pays dividends. If you know the area well, your options are apparent.

You then assume that the fish have moved from Spot A to Spot B (illustration 11). They could very easily be at Spot B hitting exactly the way they were yesterday on the same lure and same retrieve. If that doesn't work, you go through the routine a second time before you conclude that they may not have moved into the point but are hanging around the creek bend at Spot C. By knowing an area, you always stand a much better chance of catching fish.

It is equally important to remember that the bass might not be feeding, but remain schooled at Spot C because the water temperature is more to their liking or they just decide they don't want to move into shallower water to feed. There's no reason you can't catch fish at Spot C if they are there, even though the water is much deeper.

Another way to think about this hypothetical case is to consider that you caught fish early in the morning at Spot A or B. The fish were along the drop-off, but suddenly the action stopped. That's when you might want to give Spot C a try. The fish could have moved down the creek channel and right back to the U bend in the creek.

On other days, they may not be at Spot A or B at all, but you know that when they do move into shallower water, the odds are that they'll follow their own underwater highway down the creek channel.

Finally, if you find fish at a certain depth in Spot A, B, or C, you can assume that fish will also be in similar places around the lake. Check your contour map, select similar spots, and give them a thorough workout.

CREEK CHANNEL POINTS IN COVES

You already know that creek channel points are among the best places to fish, and you know that coves can also be productive. Take a close look at illustration 12 (see page 36) and study it for a few moments. The first thing you should notice on this drawing of a typical cove in a lowland- or midland-type lake is that this particular cove has six points in it. The cove also has a creek that starts back in the right-hand corner and works its way out of the cove and into the main lake.

Again, it is possible that the fish could be at any one of the points, but we're going to play the odds to maximize our fishing. That means that only those points with a creek channel nearby or that have a strong drop-off into deep water should be fished. These are always the best bets.

By looking at the drawing, you should have determined that Points #2 and #4 should be the best, because the creek channel moves right by them. That's why they are known as creek channel points. Our goal is to fish the most productive waters during the day, so, to save time, we will fish Point #2 and Point #4 only. Then we'll move on to another cove with creek channels and fish those points.

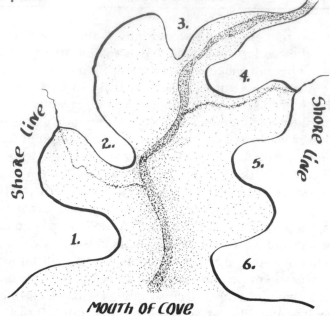

It has been our experience that we would be wasting valuable time to spend any longer in the cove unless we found some outstanding feature. This could be an underwater spring, a huge treetop, or possibly an old stump. In that case, it wouldn't hurt to give these objects a quick try. Let's say the treetop was on Point #5 and the stump on Point #3. If we made a few casts and didn't get a strike, we would pass up similar objects in the next cove and concentrate only on the creek cove points.

The reason we focus our attention on the points is simply that it is more productive to fish areas where a school of bass could be. Your chances of finding a school of largemouths on a point are a hundred times greater than finding them near a stump. A stump is usually good for only one or possibly two fish. Even during the times of year when bass aren't schooling, the creek bed points will still be the better spots and will consistently yield the larger bass.

Unless a cove is particularly large, with plenty of deep water, it will produce the greatest number of fish in the spring or fall months of the year. Coves are far more protected than the open lake; for that reason they will warm up much more quickly in the spring and cool off faster in the fall. These temperature differences between a typical cove and the main lake can be enough to attract baitfish. The bass will not only shadow the baitfish for food, but may also find the water temperatures more to their liking.

Glance at illustration 12 once more. There's a small pocket between

Points #3 and #4, where the creek enters the cove. This pocket will be the first choice for locating schooling bass when they are running bait-fish in the back end of coves. Under certain conditions, largemouths will herd shad minnows into the shallow pockets to feed, and when they do it's usually the pocket from which the creek enters the cove.

You'll also find that this same pocket will be the best for spawning bass unless it is a *running* creek. Bass don't seem to prefer a pocket for spawning if there is a lot of fresh water pouring into it. The fresh water is characteristically muddy or dingy and it is often much cooler than the lake water. Both of these factors tend to interrupt or postpone spawning.

If the creek were running into the cove, we would probably take a hard look at the pocket between Points #1 and #2, especially if there were stickups along the bank. Our plan of attack would be to work the shoreline, going down the banks in search of spawning bass. And we would do the same thing at the back end of the cove to the left of Point #3.

Any pocket that has a creek that is not running along with stick-ups is a prime area for spawning bass. You may be fishing these areas at other times of the year, but when you find those conditions, take the time to jot it down in your notebook—and remember your nota-tion the following spring when the bass invade the shallows.

Before you get the wrong idea, let us clarify our thinking on pock-ets with running creeks. Except when bass are spawning, these loca-tions can be prime bass country. Running water brings oxygen and it can mean cooler temperatures at certain times of the year. Early in the season, however, the back ends of coves warm fastest because the water is shallower and there is less wave action from the main lake. At the same time, the pocket could cool off quickly from spring rains, particularly if a creek is bringing colder water into the pocket. About the time bass feel the urge to spawn, they don't have the patience to put up with rapidly fluctuating water temperatures and will probably move into a pocket where the water is more suitable.

On a sunny day in the winter or early spring, bass can suddenly appear in the back ends of coves to take advantage of the warmer water; underwater springs that blossom in a cove will be warmer in winter and cooler in summer. Except for a bass's dislike of running creeks during spawning, that same spot might be great in the late summer or early fall when the oxygen content in the middle of the lake might provide only a narrow tier for survival, while vegetation in certain coves produces more oxygen.

The most important aspect of cove fishing is to know each cove thoroughly and then apply this knowledge to the habits of bass. When you can do that, you'll have a fair idea of when you should be concentrating on coves and when you should be over other structure.

CREEK SHOALS

Midland- and highland-type lakes are found in rolling to hilly country, and that in itself tells you that the passage of any moving water will create bluffs and shoals. Bluffs form where a creek channel swings into the bank, and shoals will form on the opposite shore. When a creek is flooded as part of an impoundment, the same type of terrain exists, except that the creek does not channel the water as it once did.

Coves with creek bluffs and shoals are great places to catch bass during the late fall, winter, and early spring. The creek, of course, enters the cove at the back end; in illustration 13 we have exaggerated the course of the creek to illustrate better how bluffs and shoals are formed. The bluff bank is normally rock, but it could very well be a high mud bank. The shoal side of the creek is always a much lower bank and is characterized by gravel, sand, or mud.

If you know that a creek enters a cove at the back end, you can almost trace the course of that creek on a midland or highland lake through the cove by looking at the banks. Where the bank is high, the creek channel moves in tight; where the bank is flat, you have a shoal, and the creek channel should be on the other side. A pass or two with a depthsounder will verify this for you.

The most productive places in this type of structure are the shoal edges, which we have marked with the letter X. This type of cove isn't the easiest to find, but when you do locate one, mark it well, because sooner or later you'll take fish on it.

Fish often will remain along the shoal edges for a considerable period of time, but just the opposite is true on the shoal points (marked Z). For some reason, bass are seldom found on the shoal points, and on the rare occasions when they are, they won't remain very long. It may be that they are on their way to another shoal edge or are ready to move back into the creek channel.

Sometimes you'll catch fish along the shoal edges and go back later only to find that the bass are gone. If you have worked the shoal edges thoroughly and even tried the shoal points without success, give the channel bed a good thrashing. It is entirely possible that the

13. Creek cove

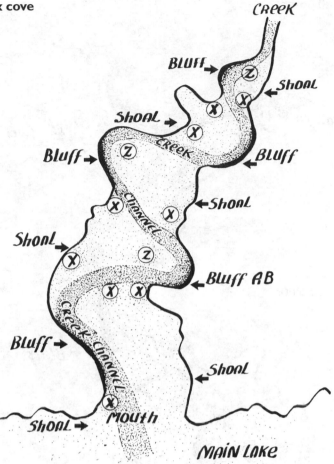

fish settled to the bottom of the creek channel at a depth that is suitable. This is especially true during the colder winter months.

It's a common mistake to think that bass won't bunch up in cold water. Not only do they bunch, but they can pack in so tightly that if you're not extremely careful, you might miss them completely. A large school of bass can occupy an area no larger than your boat.

BLUFF POINTS

Anytime you can locate a bluff point with a ledge moving out into the cove along a creek channel, you've found a hot spot that should produce fish for you over the course of time (see illustration 13, Bluff AB). We have enlarged the bluff area (illustration 14) and added some imaginary depths to help you visualize a bluff point.

14. Bluff point

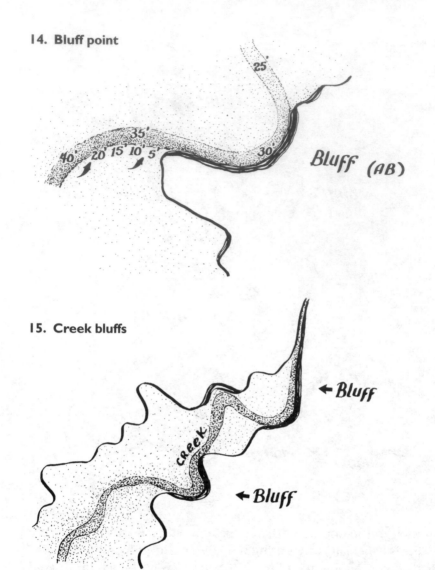

25'

35'

40' 20 15 10 5'

30'

Bluff (AB)

15. Creek bluffs

← Bluff

CREEK

← Bluff

When you find one, study the shoreline carefully and you'll get an idea of how it will look under water. The land contour above water doesn't normally change very much after it disappears beneath the surface—at least not for a reasonable distance. In our example, the bluff point forms a continuous ledge under water, moving deeper and deeper as it parallels the creek channel.

Notice how the creek gets deeper as it follows the bluff, giving you a variety of depths to fish in the immediate area. Refer to illustration 13 again and you'll see that there is another shoal area below the bluff point; this means that the bluff will slope and shoal to the left as you follow it out from the shoreline.

The bluff on the other side of the cove can also be very good if fished at the edge of the shoal, but the prime area in this cove is the bluff point. As we said earlier, we have shown a creek channel that moves from side to side for purposes of illustration. On the water, this is not always the case. There are many instances when a creek channel touches a bluff or two, forms a couple of shoals, and then moves out right through the middle of the cove (illustration 15). It would be fished the same way as we have described, only there will be fewer places to fish.

Finally, at certain periods of the year, the water level or the pool stage of a particular lake is at its low point or exceptionally low when compared to other years. This might not be a good time to fish, but you'll never have a better opportunity to explore. Get your boat as far back as you can in many of these coves and sketch the structure. Much of it could be exposed. You may even want to photograph it. When the lake fills up again, you'll have a firsthand idea of what the coves look like under water.

More on Structure

FISHING STRUCTURE and establishing a pattern require concentration and observation. You have to think your way through the problem and come up with the answers. As you become oriented to structure fishing, you will start to recognize promising spots almost automatically—and because you believe the fish are over that particular structure, you'll fish it harder and probably do much better.

Remember at all times that the prime requisite of any type of structure is the presence of deep water close by. With deep water at hand, objects such as stumps, treetops, logs, stickups, and rocks take on new meaning. An isolated weed bed can be a hot spot, and bass may be around submerged humps. A deep hole in a shallow lake could be the best spot; or lily pads, weeds, grass, or reeds might hold bass. At one time or another, bass will be on any of this structure.

CREEK OR RIVER CHANNELS

Locate a submerged creek and you know that somewhere along its length, you are going to find bass. In fact, bass will probably be at a number of locations. Remember that you should have an idea of the preferred depth for bass on that specific day, and then look for structure along the creek channel within the depth zone.

When compared to the main impoundment, the creek itself is structure, but there is also additional structure along the creek channel. It might take the form of a bend or saddle, and it would certainly be amplified by the presence of some type of cover such as weeds or brush.

Fish could be stretched along a straightaway in a creek channel, but you know that they will be concentrated along the bends, so that's the place to begin. You can locate these on a map and then pick them out easily with a depthsounder. Marker buoys will help you get the picture in a hurry.

Whether you select a U bend or S bend, the first thing to remember is that the fish will normally be on the outside bends. That's where the channel cut through, and this is part of a fish's behavior pattern if the channel weren't impounded (see illustrations 16 and 17 on page 44). If there is any cover, such as brush, on these outside bends, you can bet the fish will stay right there. If the banks are seemingly barren but there is cover a short distance away, the bass may trade back and forth from the cover to the channel.

The tighter the U bend or the S bend, the better the fishing should be. An oxbow can also be an effective place, but remember that the fish are seldom in the middle of the bend, but rather on either side of the middle. The more you know about a lake, the easier it is to find these places. If there is no cover nearby, the bass could be in the creek channel, using the submerged banks or bluffs as protection against the sun. These banks create the shadow for them, and the fish remain in the darker portion.

Another excellent place is a creek saddle, which is similar to a U bend except that the middle of the sides turn inward. They are really two outside bends that almost touch, and the fish should be between the two. Saddles are difficult to find, but they are extremely productive and worth the effort to locate. You should fish the area between the two channel segments thoroughly (see illustration 18).

When you are fortunate enough to find a saddle formed by two creeks running close together, you can start the victory celebration, because you've uncovered the greatest of all bass hangouts. When we look at a map for the first time, this is the object of our initial scanning. If the lake has two creeks that run parallel or seem to angle toward each other, we try to pinpoint this spot. It is productive nearly all the time and it is worth any effort involved to find it (see illustration 19).

You'll benefit from the flow of two separate bass populations— those that use one creek and those that use the other as a highway to move back and forth. From a fishing standpoint, you would work the area between the two creeks first; then, if for some reason that didn't produce, you might try the creek channels on the outside bends. When you find this type of structure, mark it well in your mind and notebook because you're going to want to come back to it time and time again.

Another place to find schooling bass is near the junction of two creeks (illustration 20). Usually the outside bends (marked A and B)

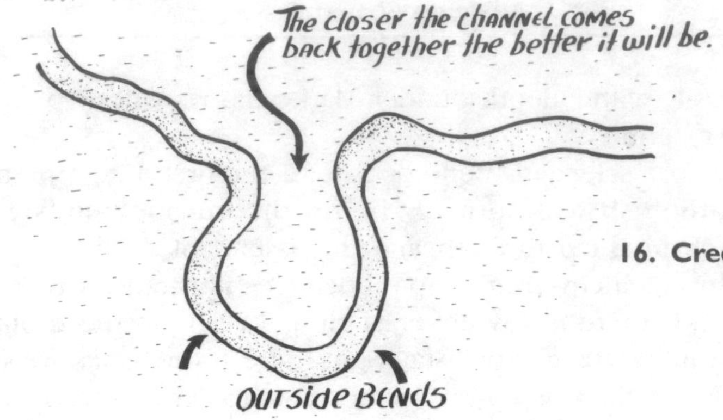

The closer the channel comes back together the better it will be.

16. Creek U bends

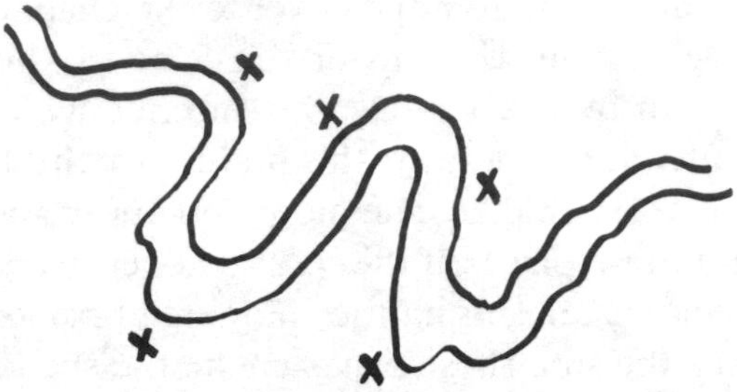

OUTSIDE BENDS

17. Creek S bends

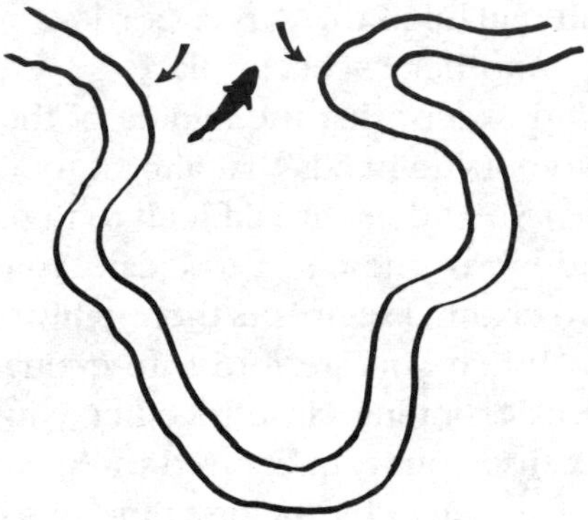

18. Creek saddle

19. A two-creek saddle

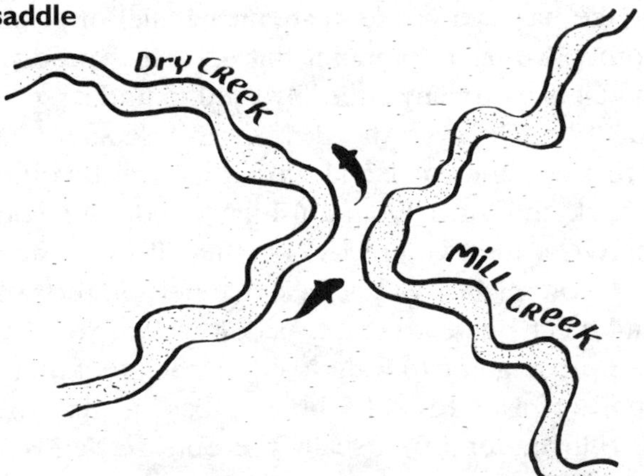

Dry Creek

Mill Creek

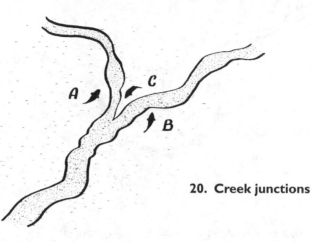

20. **Creek junctions**

are best. They will probably run along bluffs, while the shoal (marked C) is sometimes good if the depth is correct. In most cases, the shoal will be the deepest part and may hold fish if there is a drop-off on it or if the outside bends near the bluffs are too shallow or the temperature is not suitable.

Before the lake was impounded, the flow of current in the creek cut into the outside banks when the creek turned, forming a shoal opposite the bluff (see illustration 21). The bluff should have a sharper drop-off from the surface, but the bluff will also be shallower than the shoal.

When both banks of a creek channel are about the same and you don't have a bluff-and-shoal arrangement, the fish could be on either side. Your clue in this case is the amount of cover and secondary structure. Whichever side has more to offer the fish is the one the fish will be on—so study it carefully and you should come up with the answer.

If a slough, creek, or river channel runs through flat country such as under a lowland-type lake, long, flat points extending out will hold the fish (illustration 22).

We talked earlier about creek mouths and running springs, but it is worth alerting you again to their productivity, especially during certain times of the year. The key is to recognize that a flowing creek or spring will have a different water temperature from the water in the lake it enters. This means that the water near it will be warmer in winter and early spring, but cooler in late summer and early fall. Running water also produces oxygen, and this can sometimes draw fish into the area. Remember that running water indicates a temperature difference and an oxygen difference.

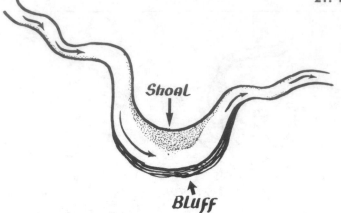

21. Bluff and shoal

22. Flat points along a lowland lake channel

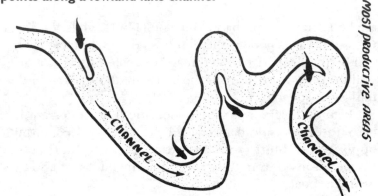

STANDING TIMBER

Standing timber is inviting structure, and it can keep the average angler busy all day just casting at the base of every tree or between the trees. To fish it properly, however, and make the most of the time available, you should have some type of plan based on experience. The most productive areas of standing timber would be near a creek channel. This channel may be along the edge of the timber or right in the thick of it, but you know you've found a highway, and if bass are moving that's the route they are going to take—and that's probably the route they'll use to leave the timber, so you can bet they'll be close by.

Take a look at illustration 23 and refer to it as we point out some of our favorite spots when fishing timber. We would probably make our first stop right where the channel enters the timber (Spot A) if

23. Key spots in standing timber

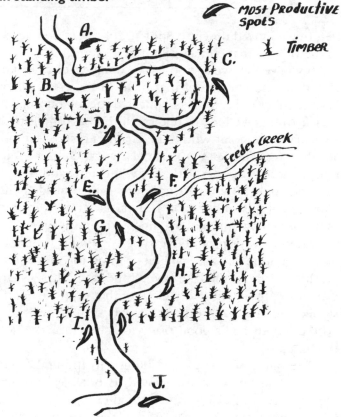

the depth is correct. Otherwise, we would pass it up and move down to the first bend inside the timber (Spot B). Spot B would be good if the bass were feeding along the timber edges. If the first bend is too far into the timber, you may want to pass it up.

Spot C is similar to Spot B, except that you have a U bend very close to the edge of the timber. Bass working this sector would most likely be right on the edge of the timber. If you don't find fish at Spot C, move on to Spot D, which is a very sharp U bend. We know from our experience with creek channels that a sharp U bend is usually a prime spot, and it would be worth checking out this part of the timber. Remember that bass would follow their normal pattern and probably stay on the outside of the U bend.

As we move down the creek channel, we find Spot E, which is an open U bend. Bass may use this as a holding place for a short time as they move back and forth between the creek junction at Spot F and the sharp U bend at Spot D. It's always worth a cast or two at the junction of two creeks, and Spot F would get that type of treatment before we moved down to Spot H. Spot G, of course, is the other side of the U bend that contains Spot E.

If you've followed us so far, you may want to make a stop at Spot H and fish the outside of that bend in the creek channel. This could be a holding point for bass, but it depends on depth and other factors. It won't take long to find out if the bass are using it.

Finally, the point where the channel comes out of the timber can also be excellent (Spot I), particularly if there is a good bend close by in open water (Spot J). Early in the morning and late in the afternoon the bass could be at Spot I, en route to the outside bend at Spot J, providing Spot J is only 50 or 100 yards away from the timber. We've seen bass follow this pattern time and time again.

Another very productive type of terrain in timber is the hump (see illustration 24). Bass will move in on top of it and take up stations on this rise above the lake floor. If the hump has a sharp drop-off, you can expect to find fish very close to that drop-off, but if it is just a high sloping area, the bass could be anywhere. Of course, they will seek the correct depth, and a good place to fish is near the heaviest cover on the hump.

The quickest way to find humps in the timber line is to look at the standing timber. If the growth is relatively the same age, simply look for trees that are standing higher than the others; chances are they appear higher because the lake bottom is higher—and that means a hump. It's not always true, but it can save a lot of time (see illustration 25).

In young timber, it may be hard to notice a difference in height among the trees, yet your map could show a high spot in that area. That means that you're going to have to check the area out with your depth-sounder to find the hump. Don't forget to mark it with buoys at least the first time to give you an idea of the physical layout of the hump.

When you're fishing timber, you should be alert to the fact that bass often show a preference for one type of tree or bush over the others. We've seen it happen time and again. With all the different species of trees in a block, the bass will hang out at the base of cedars, pines, ironwoods, sycamores, fruit trees, or something else. We can only speculate that the tree type they select grows in certain soil or gives them some favorable type of cover. The important consideration, however, is to be aware that this happens and identify the tree the moment you catch a fish. If the next fish comes from the same species of tree, then concentrate on that species right away and pass up the other trees.

24. Humps in timber

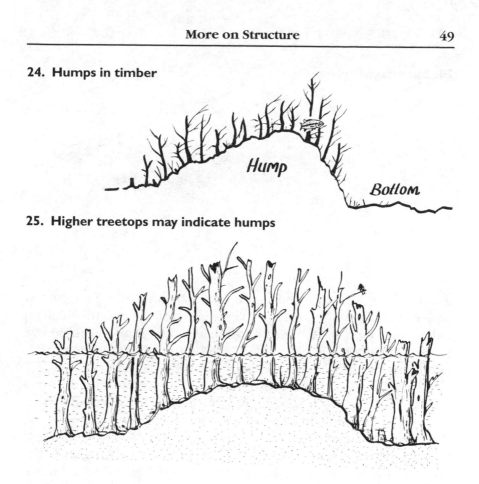

Hump

Bottom

25. Higher treetops may indicate humps

ROADS, CULVERTS, AND OTHER FEATURES

Anytime man has a hand in creating an impoundment or reservoir, it is generally in an area that was formerly inhabited. That means that there will be roads, foundations of houses, old cemeteries, and other forms of unusual structure. All these places can hold fish, and they are usually worth investigating.

Before the landscape was flooded, for example, the cemetery was moved to another location, but no one took the time to fill in the open graves. The cemetery might have been on a hillside and the open holes provide a sanctuary for bass, giving them plenty of cover and a lot of shade. Need we suggest more?

Roadbeds seem to fascinate bass and, for a reason that we can't truly explain, bass will move over the roadbed to feed. In fishing a roadbed, it is always best to look for an unusual feature: If there's a dip in the road, the bass might be right there; or they could be along

26. Submerged culvert

a curve. When the road crosses a creek channel, there's a culvert under the road, and this can be a key area. If the cover is the same on either side, you'll have to scout both sides for fish; but if there is a patch of brush on one side and nothing on the other (illustration 26), figure that the bass are in the cover and work that area first.

If the creek channel is wide enough, you know that the road would span it with a bridge rather than a culvert. The bridge may or may not be left standing, but the supports certainly will be there, and this is good structure to fish. Work the four corners where road and bridge supports meet (illustration 27), and check nearby bends in the creek channel both upstream and downstream. The fish could move into the bridge area at times and spend part of the day at the bends.

Drive along most country roads and you'll find a drainage ditch on at least one side—probably on both sides. These ditches can be great bass habitat, especially if they are filled with brush. The place to explore the roadbed and the ditches is wherever the road varies from its straight path. As we suggested a moment ago, look for dips or depressions or any spot where the road curves, and check that out first (illustration 28).

By this time, you should be well aware that you must search for the unusual aspects of structure. Stay alert to differences from the norm and then concentrate on these areas. It is impossible to outline every type of structure in detail, but we do hope that the examples we have provided will show you the things we look for when we are on the water. It won't be long before you start to develop your own patterns and theories. Just remember to record your spots and your ideas so that you have a constant source of reference for review.

27. Submerged bridge and creek channel

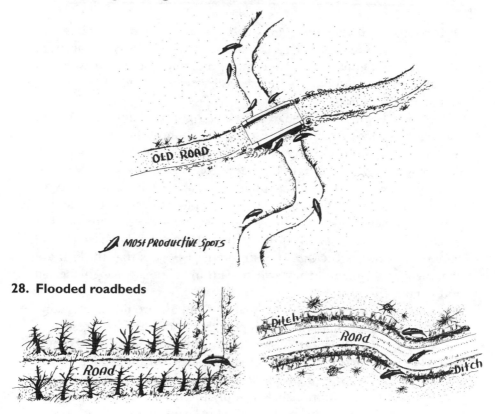

OLD ROAD

MOST PRODUCTIVE SPOTS

28. Flooded roadbeds

Road

Ditch

Road

Ditch

WHEN DO FISH SCHOOL?

We have advanced the theory that it is far better to thoroughly cover those areas where there is a chance to find a school of bass than to spend the major portion of your time snaking out a fish or possibly two from an object. This, of course, is a personal matter, and you will have to decide for yourself which type of fishing you prefer over the long haul. You can catch single fish at any of the places we have suggested, but you also have the opportunity of running into a school.

Bass spend a good part of their lives schooled up with other members of the clan; they are not necessarily the loners that some anglers make them out to be. In our judgment, bass school during at least three-quarters of the year, and they probably remain in schools for 80 percent of the time during those months.

The exception, of course, is in the springtime, when they filter into the shallows to dig nests and spawn. That's when bass refuse to be gregarious and shun their neighbors. Remember, though, that not all bass spawn at the same time, and not all bass spawn when the water temperature is best. This works two ways. It tells you that there still might be schools of bass into the springtime, and it also indicates that the spawn can continue for several weeks instead of being limited to a short period.

As soon as the females spawn, they go right back into deep water, leaving the males to guard the nest and the young. When the fry swim up for the second time and scatter, the males also move back into deeper water, and for a period of a few weeks, you just can't seem to find the larger fish. The coves, points, and shoreline boast plenty of small bass, but the lunkers are gone—probably into very deep water.

By summer, however, schools of bass start to show up, and the husky fish will reappear. You might find these schools chasing shad minnows or over structure. The important aspect is that the fish are schooled up again, and they will remain in schools through the fall and winter.

Again, we should emphasize that not all bass are doing the same thing at the same time. Even though schools of bass are present in the lake, you may have established a pattern that is producing single fish. There's no reason that you shouldn't stick with it as long as you are catching fish. One of the basic rules of fishing is never to leave fish in order to find more fish. If you ply the piscatorial pursuits long enough, you'll realize the odds are against you when you leave the fish you have found.

SUSPENDED BASS

Unless there is a current, it takes no more physical effort for a bass to sit a few inches off the bottom in 20 feet of water than it does for the same fish to suspend in treetops at the 20-foot level over perhaps 60 feet of water. Finding suspended bass is another matter. There's no other way to describe it except to note that it is an extremely difficult task.

In many cases, suspended bass are located by accident, and that is probably as good a way as any. However, there are some clues that can be gleaned, and we would like to direct your attention to them. We also reemphasize the need to hone your powers of observation and think through the problem. You must be alert to any eventuality in bass fishing and recognize it as soon as it happens.

If you've fished objects along the shoreline and structure in deeper water without catching any fish, you might suspect that some of the bass in that lake may be suspended at an intermediate level. If you're lucky, you may pick some fish up on your depthsounder, but don't count on it. When this happens, we may still fish those creek bed points, but we'll vary the technique somewhat to check for suspended bass. Instead of fishing at or near the bottom, we'll employ the countdown method and try different levels. We'll also try several lures that work in more places than just on the bottom.

Trollers can provide an excellent clue to suspended bass. If they start taking fish, you can surmise that the fish are out in the main part of the lake and that they are suspended. Work the creek bed points from both angles. Hold the boat off the point and cast in toward it, using fan casts to cover the area. Try to get the lure at various depths. Then try moving in close to shore and working out, fishing deeper and deeper. The mouths of coves are another good spot when you have an idea that bass are suspending. Don't forget to try baits that will sink, such as a tail spin, spinnerbait, spoon, and swimming bait. Count down on each cast so you know where the lure was if you should get a strike.

Bass love to suspend in timber, and show a marked preference for cedars and sometimes pines. Cedars and pines usually hold most of their limbs and provide more cover for fish than other species of trees. The bass can stay in the treetops and still enjoy the protective cover they seek (see illustration 29 on page 54).

Largemouths are particularly prone to suspend during the winter when the water is cold. They'll pack tightly in schools and will often go very, very deep in winter, but they can still be caught. As a rule, they will bunch together on the bottom and also suspend at the same depth (see illustration 30).

Bass are likely to suspend more in clear water than in murky or dingy water, and in some lakes may be in treetops at 45 or 50 feet during the chilly months. One cloudy day in the winter, we were fishing Toledo Bend, which has always been a good lake for suspended bass. The area we selected had a ledge or high spot in 25 feet of water, and we were catching bass in the 3- to 5-pound class using structure spoons and jig-and-eels. The drop-off was pronounced, and the depth plummeted sharply from 25 to 45 feet. Using our depthfinder as a guide, we hung over the drop-off, but very close to it. There were trees along this edge in 45 feet of water, and we finally started to ease up to a tree and drop either the structure spoon or the jig alongside the base of the tree.

When the lure hit bottom, we would jig it up a foot or two and

29. Suspended bass

30. School bass in winter

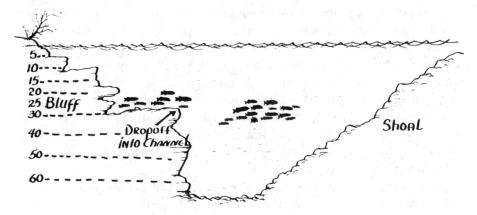

let it fall right back to the lake floor. Using this method, we happened on a good school of fish. Sometimes they would hit the lure on the first lift and other times on the fourth or fifth lift. Those fish had the trees surrounded at the bottom of the lake in 45 feet of water on a cloudy day.

You can bet we went right back there the next day and worked the base of each tree. Nothing happened. Maybe the bass were along the ledge, so we worked the entire length of that structure without a hit. Something was different today and we had to find the secret.

Then we remembered that bass will often move close to the surface in timber on a winter day when the sun is bright. They're seeking a little added warmth from the sunlight. The sun was shining brightly.

After turning the boat around and repositioning ourselves over the same spot, we quickly dropped the lure to the bottom and jigged it a few times. No fish. We then took five turns on the reel and jigged again. Still no fish. We continued doing a countdown in reverse by lifting the lure about 5 feet each time. Finally, when the lure was about 15 feet below the surface, the rod doubled over in that welcome and unmistakable arc. We had found the fish: They had moved up to take advantage of the warming rays of the sun. After that, we could use the countdown method to drop a lure to the 15-foot level where the fish would hit.

It has been our practice over the years to check for suspended fish by dropping a lure to the bottom and jigging it up in stages. This is very similar to the technique employed by fishermen who are trying to locate suspended schools of crappies. More important, before we leave an area for greener pastures, we'll usually steal a moment to try that type of retrieve once or twice. When it works, you've found the mother lode.

CHAPTER 6

Fishing the Shoreline

TRADITIONALLY, BASS FISHING has been a shoreline affair, and even the deep-water structure advocates make occasional sorties among the stumps, lily pads, fallen trees, and pockets in the banks. There's something exciting about working along the bank. Perhaps it's the constant anticipation that the dark little notch between the cypress tree and that stump next to it will produce a lunker bass. Maybe it's just the pleasure and solitude of being close to shore, listening to the many sounds, and quickening to the movement of birds and animals.

Pinpoint accuracy is especially important for this type of fishing. Being able to drop a lure exactly where you want it is part of the fun and excitement of fishing the banks—and it will produce more fish for you in the long run. Nothing is more frustrating to a shoreline fisherman than the constant need to ease into the bushes to release a lure that managed to impale itself on an overhanging limb.

READING THE BANK

The new breed of shoreline fisherman wants to have the total picture at all times. He is vitally concerned with structure along the bank, and he knows the depth at which his lure is working. If, for example, a bass crashes a bait halfway between the shore and the boat, he immediately surmises that the fish are deeper and are coming topside to catch that bait. This type of alertness is crucial to successful shoreline fishing, and it goes well beyond varying the retrieve or changing lures.

The major concept of shoreline fishing is that the configuration of the visible bank and ground behind the bank does not stop at the water's edge. It really doesn't matter whether you are fishing a man-made impoundment or plying along on a natural lake; the lake floor should be a continuation of the surrounding area. As you cruise along the shoreline, look at it closely. If you see a ridge shoulder its way across a field and bow down toward the shoreline, you can assume that it continues under the surface of the water.

There might be a gully running between two sheepbacks, and there is every indication that the gully will continue. If the bank is rocky, the rocks should also be under water. Mud shorelines usually mean mud beneath the surface. Remember we suggested that you study fields and countryside as you drive along in your car; when you do this, select an imaginary water level and then try to picture how the land would appear below that level.

Reading the shoreline will give you a good idea of what you can expect right up to the bank, and it will provide the clues to the type of structure dropping off into the deeper portions of the lake. As you fish the shoreline, you must continue to search for irregular features. They may be the edge of a tree line, the beginning of a bluff, a place where a mud bank ends and gravel begins, or anything else where a change takes place. Bass like to hang out along marginal territory where the land is changing.

THE BOTTOM

Lake bottoms are formed from a variety of materials that include mud, sand, clay, rock, gravel, grass, and even boulders. In most lakes, bottom materials change as you travel the shoreline, and they generally reflect the adjacent terrain. Look at the bank and you have a fair picture of the bottom structure. If the bank is sandy, the sand should extend into the water; and if there is small rock or gravel, the same material will be on the lake floor.

The majority of shorelines have transitional zones where mud might change to sand or gravel and rock might ease into a clay bottom. It's easy for anglers to let these changes pass unnoticed or to disregard them, but they can be prime fish habitat (illustration 31 on page 58). Bass love to lie along the transitional zone. They may feed on minnows, crawfish, and water lizards on a pebble bottom and then move just over the border to rest on a bottom formed from large rocks. When you work a shoreline, watch the bottom changes and try to relate them to a pattern. If you have a hit or hook a fish, check immediately to see if the bottom material changes; just glance at the bank and you'll have the answer.

31. Changing shoreline

Mud to Sand

1.

Rock to Sand or Clay

2.

Rock to Gravel

3.

Big Rock to small Rock

4.

Grass to Mud· Sand Rock

5.

   If you do notice that the bottom changes where you hooked your fish, this might be the beginning of a pattern. Move down the shoreline until the same condition exists again. Let's say the bottom changed from sand to grass; you fish another changeover spot and catch a second fish. Don't waste any more time puttering down the shoreline. Move directly to the next area where sand changes to grass or grass changes back to sand and fish there.

THE HOME RANGE TENDENCY

Anglers have disagreed on whether or not largemouth bass exhibit a home range tendency. That is, when the bass move into the shoreline, do they continue to occupy the same relative place repeatedly or do they pick new sections of shoreline at random, based on where they happen to be at the moment? Under the auspices of Southern Illinois

University, two scientists studied the bass population in a farm pond in Illinois and came to the conclusion that bass *do* have a home range.

The technique employed was to cover the shoreline in a boat and, using electrical shocking equipment, capture the bass on shoreline cover. The bass were then marked for identification and returned to the water. Over the course of several months, the procedure was repeated a number of times, and records kept of where each marked bass was found.

One of the more interesting facts to come from this study was that only 1.2 percent of the bass were on the shoreline at any one time, on the average. That meant that most of the bass population— over 98 percent of it—was in deep water the majority of the time. Recaptures indicated that 96 percent of the fish that did invade the shallows or shoreline were recaptured within 300 feet of the spot where they were first captured and marked for identification. With some fish, recapture took place three or four times, yet they were always within the same area. After wintering in deep water, the same bass returned to the same segment of shoreline.

BLUFFS

A bluff is a high, steep, broad-faced bank or cliff constructed of mud, clay, or rock. Bluffs are predominantly found on midland or highland lakes and often result where a creek channel works into the bank. Some bluffs have timber on them, and there are those where the timber has been cleared but the stumps are still showing. When you find a timber bluff it could be a real hot spot, and you can anticipate that although the trees may have been cut for a distance under water, some will probably remain standing in deeper water.

The best places to fish on a bluff where the creek channel comes up against it are just before the channel brushes the bank and just after the channel starts to turn away. The better spot would be the downcurrent side where the channel has moved alongside the bluff and begins to turn away. We can't tell you why the down side is better, but it is (illustration 32).

Even though a bluff can be considered structure, stay alert to the presence of what we might term "substructure." Whenever you can find structure within structure, you know it is going to be a preferred spot. This is particularly true when you are fishing a bluff, and you should look for cuts, pockets, and points on the bluff, as well as ledges or other types of cover. Bluff banks can be great places for

32. Bluff channel

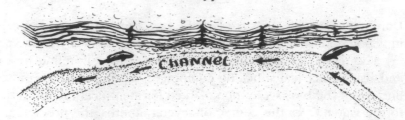

Bluff

Channel

33. Features of a bluff bank

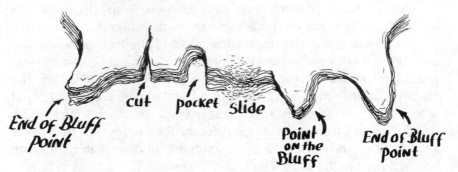

End of Bluff
Point

cut

pocket

slide

Point
on the
Bluff

End of Bluff
Point

34. Bluff ledges

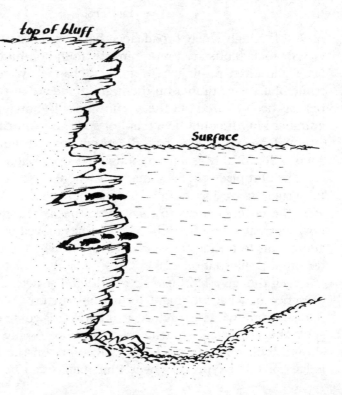

top of bluff

Surface

smallmouths, Kentucky bass, and largemouths, especially during the cold winter months (illustration 33).

Some of the most productive bluffs have ledges that extend under water. You'll see the effects of erosion above the waterline, and the strata of rock should tell you that there will be ledges under the surface. We refer to these ledges as *stair-stepped;* they are found only on rock bluffs (illustration 34). Which level the fish will occupy varies from day to day and is dictated by a combination of preferred depth and temperature; you're just going to have to experiment and work each one until you find the fish. Also keep in mind that there could be suspended fish off the ledges at approximately the same depth.

FISHING BLUFFS AND LEDGES

There is no single method for fishing bluffs and ledges. Your approach must be varied simply because old Mr. Bucketmouth is so unpredictable at times. The best way to fish a bluff—at least on the initial pass—is to parallel it (illustration 35). With a series of fan casts and the boat in a parallel position, you can fish it more thoroughly and faster than by casting into it.

If the ledges extend way out into the lake, there are times when you might want to put the boat right under the bluff and cast outward toward open water. This, of course, will move the lure from deep to shallow. We have seen times when a creek channel shoulders up to a bluff, and you could sit beyond the creek channel casting toward the bluff without a strike. Reverse the boat and cast over the creek channel from under the bluff. The fish will hit anything you throw. We mention this because direction of retrieve can be important. You should be aware that if the retrieve doesn't produce fish from one direction, it could do the job from the opposite direction.

There are other instances when the only way you're going to catch fish on a bluff is to cast directly into it and work the lure from ledge to ledge (illustration 36). Walking a lure down the ledges takes a certain amount of practice and skill; if you lift your rod tip too much, the lure will probably move too far and miss a few ledges in between. The trick is to move the lure only a few inches and let it drop a foot or two to the next ledge. If you pulled the lure a couple of feet, it might fall 10 feet before striking a ledge and you would pass up all the water between the two.

It is somewhat easier to fish the ledges at a 45-degree angle or by keeping the boat parallel. Make a cast and allow enough line for the

35. Paralleling a bluff

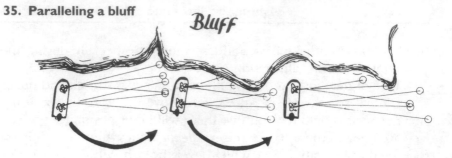

Bluff

36. Bouncing a lure down a ledge

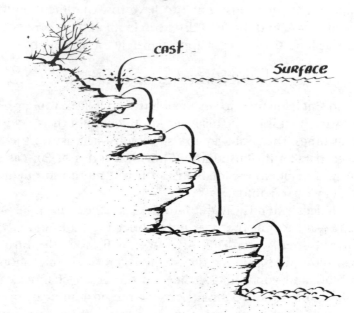

cast

Surface

jig to fall on the ledge, but follow the free fall of the lure with your rod tip. Remember, there could be suspended bass right here, and unless you watch the line you may never realize a fish picked up the lure. When the lure hits the ledge, flick the rod tip slightly and drop the lure to the next ledge. Continue the same procedure as you walk the lure down the steps.

By keeping the boat parallel to the ledges, you can also cast down one ledge and retrieve, then work the next ledge, and so forth; or you can walk the lure down the ledges on a 45-degree angle. If you do fish directly into the ledges, as we indicate in illustration 36, you must be careful that you don't drag the lure back to the boat without letting it fall to each successive level. Bouncing a jig-and-eel from ledge to ledge is not the fastest fishing method ever devised, but it is an extremely effective one and a technique that could find bass for you at any level.

SHADE

Almost every bass angler learns early in the game that bass are constantly seeking cover, and the best cover we can recommend is subdued light. For one thing, bright light seems to bother their eyes; for another, shade offers protection from predators and the advantage when feeding. A bass can hang in a shady area and gaze into a brightly lit area as if the fish were peering into a well-lit room on a dark night.

Most fishermen are visually oriented and are much more comfortable and far more confident when they can see their target. Shade offers this approach to fishing. We use the term *shade,* but we refer to *shadow* as well. Even on a cloudy day, there can be an almost imperceptible shadow coming from a bluff, tree, or rock on shore or in the water. As long as the spot you select for your next cast is a bit darker than the surrounding water, there could be fish in that spot. Make it a rule never to pass up shade. It's worth at least a couple of casts to satisfy your curiosity and perhaps that of the bass as well.

The clearer the lake, the more important shade and shadows can be. Naturally they will change as the sun swings around during the day. The fish will continue to reorient their position as the shadow line moves. Be alert to shadows, such as those from a tree or bluff, cast far out from the shoreline (illustration 37 on page 64). We have seen times when you could cast to the base of a cypress tree and hook a bass, then turn around and toss the lure into open water where the shade from that same tree offers cover. Another bass would be in the shaded patch almost 50 feet from shore.

DOCKS AND PIERS

The most noticeable feature on any shoreline is a dock or pier. In fact, it is so obvious that most anglers either overlook it or pass it up. Docks offer shade and cover, and for that reason, you'll almost always find schools of baitfish patrolling the area, darting in and out among the supports or simply under the floating docks. No one need tell you that where you find food and cover, you find bass. If it is a big dock that is used constantly, the bass might move off during the daytime when there is a lot of traffic, but they could be on hand at daybreak before any commotion begins or late in the afternoon when the last boat is tied up for the night.

Bass can be on any side of a dock or pier, but they will be back in the shade. At times they might limit their activities to the shady side

38. Dock and piers

Shadow side

SUN

(illustration 38), or they could be on the bright side but back under the dock. If your experience is similar to ours, you'll find these docks and piers best in the fall. We can't tell you why, but we know we catch more fish from this type of shoreline structure when the leaves start to turn.

If you don't limit your bass fishing simply to casting the shoreline, there's one other aspect of docks and piers that you should keep in mind. Study a contour map of the marina and dock sites. If there is a creek channel or a deep hole nearby, the bass might stay there during most of the day, moving into the dock area at dawn and again at dusk. It's worth a try to locate deep structure near a dock. Most anglers are too busy heading for the other end of the lake.

Launching ramps are another place frequently passed up. Bass will sometimes move right up on the concrete ramp, or they could stay right along the edges. Most ramps drop off into relatively deep water, so the escape routes are right there.

In fishing docks, piers, or ramps, you can use almost any type of lure that you would normally fish, and you'll soon learn that docks that have brush piled under them or nearby are better choices.

DAMS AND RIPRAPS

The area around a dam is often a favorite haunt of the bait fisherman, but it can also be productive for the artificial-lure enthusiast. The key is to look at the dam as shoreline structure, taking maximum advantage of shadows, water flow (if there is any), channels, cuts, sloughs, and the edges where the dam meets the shoreline.

You can alternate your fishing from shallow to deep and deep to shallow. If the water channel cuts an edge along a shoal, you may want to parallel it and fan cast. When water is being pulled through the dam, baitfish are sometimes taken along for the ride, or at least they become disoriented in the flow of water. Bass could be on the prowl just out of the main current, picking off the hapless minnows as they struggle against the water flow. Moving water also carries more oxygen, and this could be an important consideration during the warm months, when oxygen content could become critical.

Ripraps are rock walls that help to hold back the water on the sides of a dam or where a bridge might cross the impoundment. They are designed to resist erosion. When these walls were constructed, the basic material came from the lake bottom. That means that there will be a trough or a drop-off nearby.

You can fish a riprap in any one of three ways. The most common approach is to hang over the deeper water and cast the lure into the riprap. If you prefer this method, try some casts at a 45-degree angle as well as straight in to the target. You may also want to parallel the riprap, casting up and down. Be particularly alert to the corners of the riprap, where it joins the normal shoreline. If all else fails, you could get out of the boat and walk along the riprap, casting on a 45-degree angle and straight out into the deeper water. Very often a riprap wall can be fished better from shore than from a boat.

When you fish this type of structure, be alert to other forms of substructure. Perhaps you find a break in the wall or a minor slide where some rocks fell into the water. Maybe it's a log or a stump or simply a large rock. Whatever the substructure, it's worth your time because, if fish are along the wall, they should be near the substructure.

STUMPS

Of all the objects in the water, none seems to arouse the confidence of a bass fisherman more than an exciting-looking stump. For some reason, we all associate largemouths with stumps. On the other hand, some stumps can be more productive than others. As an example, a stump that sits on the edge of a drop-off will usually be better than a stump way back up in the shallows, if the depth is correct. When we say *usually* better, we mean on a consistent basis rather than a single experience (illustration 39).

Remember that the shady side of an object is normally better than the brighter side. Therefore, your first cast should always explore the shady side. At one time, bass fishermen always tried to drop a lure right on the object they were fishing. If the object was a stump, they would try to hit the stump on the cast and let the lure fall alongside. By doing this, they passed up a lot of productive water behind and alongside the object, and the sound of a lure falling over the head of a bass could spook the fish into deep water (illustration 40).

We prefer to make our first cast on the side and beyond the object. Sometimes a bass won't be right on the object, but near it. By casting in this manner, we can cover the back, side, and front with a single cast. Once the lure passes the object and is well on its way toward the boat, you might as well crank it in and cast again. Big bass will seldom follow a lure any distance. If they want your offering, they'll hit it as it comes by.

You can fish a variety of lures around stumps. Topwaters, spinnerbaits, worms, jig-and-eels, swimming lures, and diving lures can all be good choices. You're going to have to experiment to find out which ones are best for you. Keep in mind that you may have to vary the retrieve to catch fish. We have seen times when we can cast a spinnerbait past a stump and buzz it by quickly; a bass would nail it before it even reached the stump. The next day in the same area the bass wouldn't hit a spinnerbait unless we buzzed it up to the stump, stopped the lure dead, and let it fall. They would have it in their mouth before it dropped a foot.

The second cast around a stump should still be beyond it, but the lure should brush the object as it passes. There's no guarantee that a bass will hit your lure on the first or second cast, even if the fish is right there. You may have to cast six or eight times before you get a strike, and change lures in the process. That's bass fishing, and there is no shortcut to success.

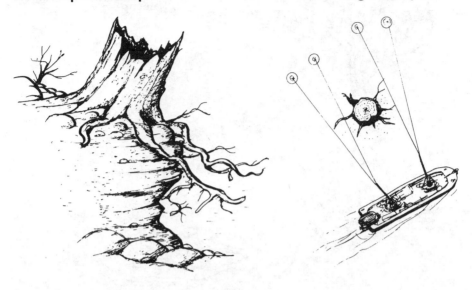

TREES

Some old-timer once theorized that "if you ain't hangin', you ain't fishin'." When he uttered those immortal words, he must have been talking about treetops, because it is easy to hang up in this type of structure. If trees are left standing, the branches may protrude above the surface, or they could be just under the surface. The way we prefer to work a treetop is from the branches to the trunk (illustration 41).

Start with a spinnerbait and buzz it through the branches. You know, of course, that those trees with more branches and limbs offer better cover for bass and should be fished first. After you've tried the spinnerbait across the top, you could let it drop in the branches and work it carefully. Another choice would be to make a commotion with a topwater bait around the edges of the branches and then toss a worm into the middle of the limbs, letting it fall around the cover. Considerations include the time of year, clarity of the water, depth of the tree, preferred temperature, and similar factors. It's almost impossible to list all the variables, but you know from the previous chapter that, on a sunny day in winter, the bass could be right up near the top of the tree.

If the tree is under water, you might want to get the boat right over the top and use a structure spoon, if the time of the year is right. Or you could choose a fall bait and work it right down around the base of the tree. There's no single formula, but we hope these suggestions will trigger ideas of your own.

Shallow-water, light-tackle saltwater fishermen learned the value of

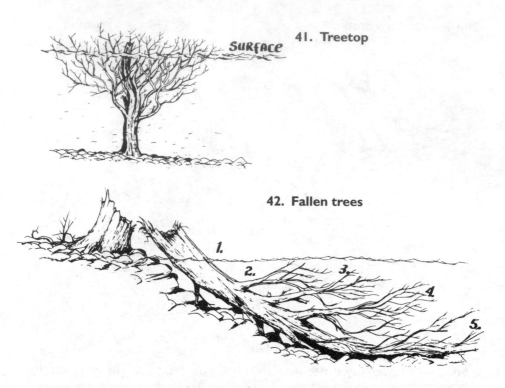

41. Treetop

SURFACE

42. Fallen trees

1.
2.
3.
4.
5.

polarized sunglasses a long time ago. They make quite a difference in looking through the surface of the water, and they can be invaluable in spotting objects below the surface. They are not miracle glasses, but rather a type of glass that eliminates surface glare, enabling you to see better.

Frequently, a tree blows down in a storm or rots out and comes crashing into the water. All that remains on the bank or in the shallows is a stump and a short end of the tree base (illustration 42). The spot looks perfect, and it probably is. Most fishermen will immediately begin to cast around the stump and the portion of the tree protruding above the surface, but for some reason, the average angler will totally ignore the fact that the rest of that tree is probably under the surface. The part of the tree extending above the surface can give you an idea of the underwater terrain. If it seems to stand almost straight up (upside down), you know that there is a major drop-off. If the log appears to lie flat, you'll probably see the branches at the other end and know that a drop-off isn't present.

It's not always easy to tell if there are limbs and branches left on the deep end of the tree, but it is certainly worth investigating. There are several different ways that this structure can be fished. If you are using a topwater bait, start a series of fan casts from the stump and stub of the tree across the area where the rest of the tree should lie.

43. Fishing a blowdown or fallen tree

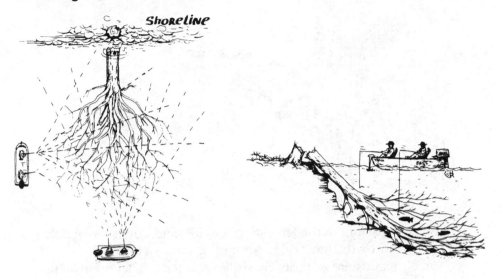

Then switch to a spinnerbait and follow the same series of casts, allowing the lure to fall deeper on each succeeding cast (from the shallow end to the deep end). You might also try a jig-and-eel or a worm and toss it back into the section of the tree that has branches.

Once you know that a particular blowdown has branches, a better way of fishing it is to position the boat out in deep water and fan cast along the length of the tree. The idea is to cast into the tree and retrieve in the direction the branches point. By doing this, you will minimize the chances of hanging up (illustration 43).

If the tree plummets almost straight down, you may want to electric-motor over it and use a structure spoon or jig-and-eel to probe the bottom branches. Each tree should be analyzed individually and fished according to time of year and the way it lies in the water.

STICKUPS

Stickups don't provide very much cover for a bass, but they are significant structure in the spring when the bass move into the shallows to spawn. At that time, the fish are willing to sacrifice habit and ignore cover. One reason is that bass require sunlight in spawning, at least to keep the water warm so the eggs will hatch in the normal length of time. Rather than just stay out in the open, the bass will shoulder up to a stickup. Stickups on hard bottoms such as sand or gravel are usually the most productive.

A plastic worm or a spinnerbait is relatively hangproof and is an excellent choice for this type of fishing. The best way to cover a

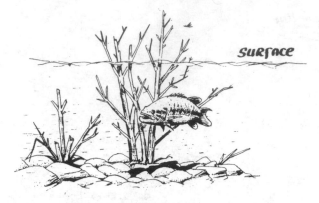

stickup is by casting to the left side, right side, and down the middle. If a bass is nearby, the lure will be seen (illustration 44).

Since stickups are in relatively shallow water, a quiet approach is necessary; any noise from a motor or noise that is transmitted through the hull will chase the fish into deeper water. However, since the fish are either spawning or guarding the nest when they are among the stickups, they are very aggressive and will come back quickly.

TILTED LOGS

Anytime you see a log in open water with one end reaching above the surface, you can assume that the log is waterlogged on the larger end and has floated up against a ledge or drop-off. It's a good visual clue to structure and certainly worth investigating (illustration 45). The fish may be near the log, or other parts of the drop-off could be even more productive.

To fish a tilted log, apply about the same approach as you would use on a fallen tree. The log may or may not have limbs left on it, but

45. Tilted logs

you can determine this by working a lure through the deeper portion. If there are limbs, you'll feel a lure brush by. And you could also use a structure spoon in this type of situation.

Lily Pads

The terms *bass* and *lily pads* are almost synonymous. From the time a youngster begins his fishing career, he learns that bass hang out around the lily pads waiting for a minnow, frog, or crawfish to happen by. Lily-pad fishing requires a lot of patience, because there are usually large areas of pads and it takes time to find the fish. Pads grow in the shallows, which makes the area somewhat sensitive and dictates a quiet approach.

Take a look at illustration 46 on page 72. We have created a typical lily-pad setup, and experience has shown that there are certain areas among the pads more prone to hold fish than are other areas. Concentrate your fishing on these key spots and then move on to the next set of pads. If you happen to establish a pattern in the pads, then you would naturally fish your pattern in every set of pads you could find.

You already know that anywhere there is a change in the shoreline or the bottom material changes, you could find bass. The same theory holds true when lily pads are present. There could be fish at Spots 1 and 10, where the pads start and where they stop. Try the corners and then move out to the first major point, indicated as Spot 2. Spot 8 would be the first point if you approached the pads from the other direction and could be equally good, regardless of whether you were fishing the shoreline from right to left or left to right.

When you find a small pocket reaching back among the pads, it can produce a fish or two and is worth a few casts. Spot 3 is typical of this type of structure among lily pads. One or two points that extend farther into the lake might also be good (Spot 4). Work either side of the point and back into those pads.

When you've found a pocket going back into the pads from the outer edge, give it a good working over. Spot 5 shows this type of pocket, and it should be fished at the points on either side as well as the mouth. Then you can move into the pocket and fish it. Any tiny offshoots such as Spot 6 warrant a cast or two.

Many assortments of lily pads have small circular openings completely surrounded by pads. It's tough to get a fish out of this type of real estate, but you can certainly get it to hit. Cast back and across these openings and work the lure through them.

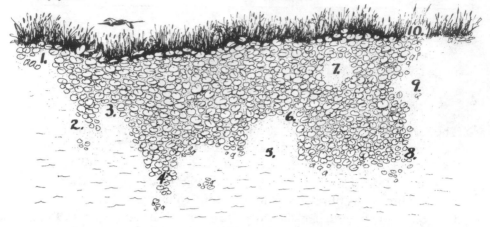

Finally, don't forget to consider the direction of the sun. Indentations on the shady side, such as Spot 9, could harbor a fish. You can easily spend most of the day around a set of pads, but the better approach is to concentrate on the highlights and high spots and then move on to different structure or another set of pads.

LURES FOR LILY-PAD FISHING

The old standby for lily-pad fishing is a spoon, dressed with a pork rind or plastic skirt. These weedless spoons come with weedguards that enable you to drag the lure tantalizingly across the surface of the water, or you can let it sink and snake it through the pad stems. You have a choice of colors in both the spoons and the tails, and it is sometimes worth experimenting with a couple of different color combinations, such as a light spoon and then a dark one. When a bass hits this lure, come back on it hard and fast to set the hook; strike instantly.

Plastic worms are another good bait for lily-pad fishing, and they can be rigged with or without a slip sinker. You can crawl a worm from lily pad to lily pad, pausing to let it rest and then slither off a particular pad; or you can use a slip sinker and let it fall beneath the pads, fishing it like a weedless spoon. When a bass hits the worm in the pads, pause a second before setting the hook.

The weedless frog is an old-time lure that has taken its share of bass. It's basically topwater and should be fished around the pads as well as on top of them. You can pop it up on a pad and let it sit there for several seconds before moving it off. Do this two or three times and a bass might surprise you when it plasters the lure by blasting right up through the lily pad and eating pad and lure at the same time.

Of course spinnerbaits are a good bet in the lily pads, because they are basically weedless and can be worked in a variety of retrieves. You might want to buzz the spinner across the top of the pads or allow it to sink. Combine both retrieves by buzzing and stopping until you find the formula. When the extended wire on the spinnerbait comes back beyond the hook, it is much more weedless than spinnerbaits with shorter-span wires.

Unless a topwater lure is weedless, the angler who prefers this type of surface action will have to limit his activity to the edges of the pads and pockets or openings. Topwater fishing can also be used to explore the pad points. This gives the topwater devotee plenty of area to explore, and the commotion from such a lure could bring bass out from deeper in the pads.

Swimming and diving plugs suffer the same basic limitations as top-waters. They can be used to work the fringes of the pads, but toss one back into the thick of things and you'll have to motor over to get it out.

You've probably shared with us the experience of finding bass way back in the pads when the cover was just too heavy to drag a bass out. We've had our share of frustrations with this type of fishing, and on occasion we'll run the boat back into the pads, cutting them with the motor. That leaves an open pocket, but of course the bass have scattered. So we'll leave this honey hole for a while and come back several hours later to fish the new pocket we created. Not surprisingly, we'll catch bass.

How to Fish
an Unfamiliar Lake

A N UNFAMILIAR LAKE may be one that you have fished for a number of years and never really taken the time to learn, or it could be a body of water that is completely new to you and one that you are going to try for the first time. Some writers refer to this situation as "fishing a strange lake," but we believe that there is nothing strange about any lake that harbors largemouth and smallmouth bass.

It's all a matter of mental attitude. Even the finest bass masters sometimes experience difficulty on new waters, because they are overwhelmed by new and unfamiliar surroundings, thus failing to place the problem in its proper context. If you think for a moment, you'll realize that there will be many similarities between the new water and your favorite bass lakes. Equally important, you can expect the bass to follow the same habits and seek the same habitat it does anywhere else. Just because the physical layout of an impoundment changes doesn't mean that the characteristics of the species undergo a metamorphosis.

If you have analyzed the new lake carefully, you already know that bass will seek a preferred depth based on temperature and oxygen. Add to that the requirements for food and cover and it shouldn't be too difficult to locate your quarry. All that is left to do is find the structure and features of the new water that are most likely to hold bass.

START WITH A CHART

To fish an unfamiliar lake properly, you're going to need a chart or map to help you locate the type of structure that bass frequent. If your fishing is limited to shoreline casting, a detailed map or chart will still help you to find such areas of different soil consistencies as hills and creeks. As a general rule, always try to obtain a map with the smallest depth intervals. A 5-foot interval, for example, is always better than an interval of 10 or 20 feet. It might take several different maps to provide the information you need, including a navigational map, Corps of Engineers map, and Geological Survey map.

In addition to the maps, you will need a good temperature gauge that reads the water temperature at various depths electronically, and a depthsounder capable of displaying the bottom at realistic boat speeds.

Before you even depart for the new lake, study the maps carefully, trying to pick out features that could hold bass. Primarily, you are looking for structure, so concentrate on finding creeks, submerged channels, roadbeds, field flats, humps, high spots, old home foundations, and anything else you can find that is different from the surrounding area.

If you know a marina operator or a guide on the lake you're going to fish, a telephone call in advance can help you obtain information on the depth the fish are being taken at. Once you know the depth, spread your maps out in front of you and start to mark all the structure you can find that conforms to that depth. Perhaps you won't be able to pinpoint the depth exactly, but your own experience might tell you that most bass in that part of the country and at that time of year are taken in 12 to 20 feet of water. You can use that information to locate structure within the given range.

SELECT A SMALL AREA

There is a tendency among bass anglers with superfast boats (and even among some who own slower boats) to attempt to cover too much territory. They'll fish one spot, then crank up and run for another spot that might be 8 or 10 miles down the lake. Much of their fishing time is spent in running from spot to spot, with the result that they fail to cover any area thoroughly. The secret of finding fish in any lake is to maximize the time that your lure is in the water.

On an unfamiliar lake, study the chart until you have selected a few areas that seem to have the best potential. The lake may be 50 miles long or it could be 10 miles long, but that's still too much territory to try to cover. Instead, pick an area of possibly 4 miles that looks as if it has plenty of structure with creeks running through it. Mark every spot you can find in this limited zone on the chart, noting water depth. Three or four different-colored marking pens can help you establish a depth code. Red might mean 12 to 15 feet, blue could be 16 to 20 feet. That will help you pick out depths quickly.

Instead of running all over the lake to fish this place or that, our approach is to concentrate on the limited area we selected and fish it hard. If you don't have exact depth information, you can use your temperature gauge as an indicator, or you can fish a sloping point until you catch the first fish and then measure the depth.

ESTABLISH A PATTERN QUICKLY

Most bass anglers fish an unfamiliar lake as part of a vacation trip or business excursion; often they won't be in the area very long, and if they are going to catch fish they must do so quickly. That means that the visiting angler must establish a pattern as soon as possible. Remember that there may be several patterns that will work at any one time, but you need only uncover one.

The more familiar you are with a lake, the easier it is to fish, so you must recognize this fact when you fish an unfamiliar lake and take extra measures to ensure you have found the right structure. Triangulation will help you pinpoint spots in midlake, and your depthsounder will confirm them. If you are going to fish a high spot or a creek channel or any other type of structure, don't skimp on putting out marker buoys. They'll help you to get oriented in the shortest time.

If, for example, you are going to fish a U bend in a creek channel, it may take 8 or 10 markers to delineate the bend, but it is worth the time crossing and crisscrossing the channel to drop the buoys. Then, when you look at it, you'll have a better idea where to fish. And if you do take fish in, say, 20 feet of water, pull out your map and see if there is another U bend in 20 feet of water. That's the next place you want to fish.

There's very little that is different when you fish an unfamiliar lake other than the physical features. If you can't catch fish using the techniques you know and the lures that you can work best, you probably won't have time to learn a new method.

DEEP, CLEAR LAKES

Some of the best bass anglers in the country have had their share of problems with deep, clear lakes. Those fishermen who live near lakes of this type quickly tell you that the problem is strictly mental and results in a defeated frame of mind. An angler who can't miss on a shallow lake begins to think that he doesn't know anything about deep lakes. Mention that the water might be 200 feet deep in places and this veteran will go to pieces.

The truth of the matter is that you are only going to look for fish down to depths of possibly 35 feet or so. When you are fishing 35 feet of water, it is no different than fishing the bottom of a lake that is only 35 feet deep. All you have to do is ignore the deeper water and concentrate on the shallower sections. Once you do that, the deep, clear lake becomes like any other body of water you have fished.

Clear water, of course, means that the fish will probably be a shade deeper than they might be in dingy or murky water, so you would fish slightly deeper than you normally might, but that doesn't mean you have to fish depths of 50 or 60 feet. And you'll find that in clear water, lighter lines and smaller lures result in more fish.

Working the Shoreline

You may not be the type of fisherman who enjoys fishing structure in deeper water, preferring to do your bass catching along the shoreline. The shoreline of an unfamiliar lake is basically the same as any other length of shoreline. It will have special features that will hold bass, and your job is to recognize these features.

Bass might hang out where gravel turns to mud, or where a bluff ends and a shoal starts. Fish might be along submerged timber, or at key points among the lily pads. The point to remember is that even though you are fishing the shoreline, you must remain alert to changes in terrain and try to establish a pattern.

The alternative is to waste a lot of time dropping a lure along every stump, every undercut bank, and anywhere else that looks as if it might harbor a bass. Points are always worth a few casts, and anyplace where running water enters a lake could prove productive. If you do uncover a pattern, stick with it and pass up places that don't fit that pattern. Otherwise, you could be spending too much time fishing unproductive waters.

Lakes without Structure

There are some lakes that simply cannot be structured. The underwater configuration of these lakes resembles a bowl or a frying pan. If you were to drain the water out of the lake, the bottom would be relatively smooth without much in the way of cover or drop-offs. However, unless you think your way through the problem, locating bass in water of this type could be like searching for the proverbial needle in the haystack.

A lake not too far from home fits the bowl-shaped description, and although it holds some husky bass, there is no way to locate these fish consistently except in the spring when they are spawning in the shallows. If we can locate a depression in the bottom one of these days, it should be filled with bass like a "hawg pen," but so far that lake bottom is completely level.

In a lake without visible structure, it is important to remain particularly observant. Subtle changes such as a sand-to-gravel bottom or a certain species of tree might hold the key to locating the bass. Every time a fish is taken, study the spot carefully and try to pinpoint the salient features. When the next fish is hooked, look for duplication of certain features; if you find some that occurred in the first spot, you may be on to a pattern.

Finally, keep in mind that in a lake without significant structure, even a minor change in the bottom can be enough to hold fish. So stay alert to a change of any type in a bowl-shaped or frying-pan-shaped lake.

LOCATING TROPHY SMALLMOUTHS

Show most bass anglers a patch of rocky shoreline or a rocky point extending out into the lake and their first thoughts center on smallmouths. This may hold true for smaller specimens, but the husky smallmouths prefer a different type of terrain.

Spring and fall are the best times to fish for smallmouths. Dale Hollow Reservoir in Tennessee, for example, begins to turn over in late November when the water temperature ranges between 58° and 54° F. That's also the time when smallmouths move over the "flats" and begin to school in 18 to 35 feet of water, and they will remain at those depths until the water temperature dips below 45° F.

If you've been concentrating on rocky points for your smallmouth fishing, you've been looking for trophy fish in the wrong places. These fish are not in the fishy-looking spots, but over relatively clean bottom composed of clay, mud, or gravel. That's where the crawfish feed and that's where the smallmouths will be, since the crawfish is the mainstay of their diet. In fact, if a lake doesn't have a superb supply of crawfish, it probably won't hold trophy smallmouths, because smallmouths grow faster on crawfish than on any other food.

In deep lakes, most banks drop off sharply. You can tell this by studying the shoreline. Check the shore until you find a ridge or hump that tapers gradually to the water's edge. You'll probably see mud or clay at the water's edge. If this bank continues to extend gradually into the lake, it could be trophy smallmouth territory. Prime smallmouth country is a gradually tapering point that eases out into the lake with plenty of deep water all around it. Smallmouths require deep water nearby and, although they'll work the edges of the tapering points, they demand the safety of the depths.

Until you get to know a lake, you must rely on a depthsounder to help you find the gradually tapering points. The best method is to locate the muddy points that look flat on shore and then check them out with the depthsounder. If they drop into 35 feet of water or more, they are worth fishing. However, trophy-sized smallmouths can be difficult fish to approach, and they spook easily. If you have worked a point with a depthsounder or dropped buoys, you won't be able to fish it until the next day; the best approach is to spend your first day scouting the most likely-looking smallmouth spots and then return the next day to begin fishing.

OBSERVATIONS ON SMALLMOUTHS

One reason largemouths are much easier to approach and fool than smallmouths is that smallmouths respond unfavorably to the presence of a boat or the glimpse of an angler. Don't for a moment delude yourself into thinking that fish can't see you, even in deep water!

In approaching a point that might have smallmouths, the trick is to move in as quietly as possible. Ease the throttle on your big motor some distance from the spot you want to fish, so that a heavy wake doesn't roll over the area. Then work in from the side you don't intend to fish and get the boat right up against the bank. You generally work from the shallow to the deep, so your lure will be pulled up the point from the deep to the shallow. Fish seem to hit it better in this direction, and it is much easier to keep the bait near the bottom.

With the boat near the bank, make a series of fan casts, retrieving the lure slowly so it is just off or bouncing along the bottom. When you have covered the sector, ease the boat into deeper water about half the length of a long cast and repeat the fanning. Move again and cast the new area. Most anglers don't work deep enough on these points, and it is good to remember that, although the fish might be a little shallow early in the morning or on an overcast day, they could just as well be in 30 feet of water.

When fishing over these flat points, always cast as far as you can. The bait should be allowed to sink to the bottom, and you must remain alert while the bait is falling (maintaining a tight line), because a smallmouth could inhale it on the way down. If a fish doesn't strike, the retrieve should be painstakingly slow, permitting the lure to skim the bottom. You can check the depth of retrieve by periodically dropping your rod tip. The lure should hit bottom within the count of two or three, or you're fishing it too fast and too high.

Smallmouths are creatures of habit, living in the same places year after year after year. Once you find good smallmouth territory, the schools will be there next year at the same time. They don't range very far during the entire year, moving deeper or shallower with the seasons.

During the middle of winter in lakes such as Dale Hollow, the smallmouths will be very deep. If you have a calm day, you may be able to fish them in 50 or 60 feet of water. However, with the first warm rains in March, the smallmouths can move shallower overnight and start to feed. During March, April, and early May (depending on the latitude), they'll move into the shallows in search of food, and they'll also spawn. Smallmouths usually spawn in slightly deeper water than largemouths, and how close they get to shore depends on the amount of cover available. If you have always wanted to catch a big smallmouth on a fly, this is the time of year to do it, but you must make long casts and approach the nests or the cover very quietly and carefully.

Finally, the clearer the lake, the lighter the line you should be using. You'll catch more fish in clear water on 6-pound test than you will on 10-pound test; and you'll discover that by eliminating terminal tackle, such as swivels, and using a small bait, you'll increase your chances of hooking a trophy smallmouth. Just remember that big smallmouths prefer small baits worked slowly along the bottom. They may occasionally hit a larger offering, but that's the exception.

STRIPED BASS—AN UNFAMILIAR SPECIES

The striped bass is primarily an anadromous species of inshore gamefish in salt or brackish water, which means that it moves up into fresh water to spawn. It is closely related to the white bass, but grows extremely large. Fish over 20 pounds are not uncommon in freshwater impoundments, and there have been some taken over 40 pounds. The striper can be a tough adversary on the end of the line, but the problem is understanding the habits and habitat of this species.

Characteristically, stripers respond differently based on the seasons of the year. When water temperatures drop below 48° F, the striped bass begins to get sluggish and will often hang suspended over deep holes in a semidormant state. As the water begins to warm in the early spring, these bass will move into shallower water and over large flats prowling for food. They are primarily feeding on the bottom at this time of year, and the best way to take them is on cut or live bait. If you want to fish artificials, the choice lure would be a small white bucktail bounced slowly on the bottom.

After stripers spawn in mid-May or early June, they begin to school and will stay in schools through the balance of the year. That's the time when you can really do a job with artificials. Stripers are predators and will either hang around brush piles where they can pounce on unsuspecting prey or cruise the drop-offs of large flats extending out into the lake. Pattern depth is tough to determine, but you can generally estimate it at between 15 and 25 feet. Often, they will move right up on the flats to feed. These shallow bars are normally 5 to 10 feet deep.

To locate stripers, the first thing you do is study a map of the area. Look for large flats with 5 to 10 feet of water that extend out into the lake. Then search for a drop-off. If you can find brush along the drop-off, you can often find stripers. That's where your depthsounder will come in handy. One way to use it is to cruise the edge of the drop-off looking for brush. If you do this, be certain to zigzag, because the brush could be just beyond the drop-off, and your depthsounder won't pick it up unless you run right over the top of it.

Another way to locate brush (and this one works even if you don't have a depthsounder) is to drift or electric-motor along the edge of the drop-off. Make long casts with a heavy lure such as a structure spoon like the Hopkins #75. Let the lure sink to the bottom and retrieve it slowly. You are actually trying to hang it up in brush. If the lure hangs, ease over, work the lure loose, and fish the area.

Standing timber also can provide a home for stripers, and you'll find the fish among the branches quite regularly. We had great striper fishing in some standing timber on Tennessee's Percy Priest Lake, with largemouths thrown in as icing on the cake.

Perhaps the best way to take stripers out of brush is with a structure spoon. The technique is to move over the brush pile with an electric motor and lower the spoon over the side. Let it fall freely, but control the drop with your rod tip. You must achieve a delicate balance in which the lure is unimpeded as it drops, but the line is tight enough to tell you if the lure is stopped on the way down. Any back pressure on the lure caused by not allowing it to fall at its natural rate will destroy the action and hinder the catching of striped bass.

When the lure hits the bottom, lift it off by moving the rod tip upward. Normally, you want to lift the lure from 4 to 6 feet off the bottom and then allow it to fall back again, using your rod tip to follow the line down. Every strike will occur as the lure falls, so watch the line carefully. You may not always see or feel the strike until you start the next lift, but you can bet the fish took the lure on the fall.

Because you're fishing right in the brush, you'll need fairly heavy line and a rod with enough backbone to move the striper out of the obstructions. Some anglers use lines as heavy as 25-pound test, but this is a matter of experience and personal preference. You can probably get by with something a little lighter if you can get on a fish quickly and wrestle the critter out of the bushes.

Frequently, you'll see schools of breaking stripers herd shad and feed ravenously. When this happens, you can join the action with bucktails or plugs. Some of the best lures are smaller versions of the striper plugs that are popular along the Northeast Coast. The trick in this situation is to match the size of your lure to the size of the shad or other minnows on which the bass are foraging. If the shad are 10 inches long, use a 10-inch plug. If they are 4 inches long, your lure should be 4 inches.

White bucktails are also a very good choice for catching striped bass, and you can sometimes improve their efficiency by taking a felt-tipped marking pen (permanent type, not water soluble) and coloring in a green wing on each side of the white bucktail. Stripers, for some reason, like white bucktails with green wings, and it is often easier to color an all-white model than to find or tie one with the two colors.

When you retrieve a bucktail, resist the tendency to sweep the rod tip and impart action. Instead, cast out into the fish and reel steadily, without any additional action from the rod. We saw this fact proven again and again during some experiments on Oklahoma's Keystone Reservoir. With stripers covering acres of a shallow flat, we cast into their midst and proceeded to use the rod to impart action to the bucktail. Nothing happened. Then we reeled steadily without any action and a striper would hit it every time. Not satisfied, we went back to the action-type retrieve, and the fish would ignore the bucktail.

Striped bass are always great sport when you can find them, but knowing a little about their habits and how to catch them can often save the day when the largemouths are uncooperative. From June through December, it pays to carry a few structure spoons with you, along with some white bucktails. If there are stripers in the impoundment you are fishing, mark the drop-offs on your map and start exploring them.

CHAPTER

Farm Ponds

A GREAT MANY anglers enjoyed their first taste of bass fishing on a farm pond, small soil-conservation lake, or miniature watershed lake, and these mini waters still produce some of the finest bass fishing in the country.

The point to remember about farm ponds is that they are really small lakes, and they possess the same characteristics as larger lakes and impoundments. Known in Texas as tanks, these ponds might be 2 acres or 80 acres; some are clear, others are muddy; and some have creek channels running through them, others don't.

Because the farm pond is smaller than a large impoundment, the bass are easier to locate. However, farm ponds can have as much structure as their larger cousins, and you'll quickly discover that some areas of the pond are consistently more productive.

Not only do farm ponds produce excellent bass fishing, but they are a great training ground for learning more about the habits of a bass. Because the waters cover less area, it's easier to find structure in the deeper parts, and you can begin to get the feel of structure fishing. If you think of a pond as the small area of a large impoundment you decided to fish, this will help you to get oriented.

The first step in fishing a farm pond (since you probably won't find a depth-information map on the pond) is to talk to the landowner. It's always important to ask permission to fish these waters but, equally significant, he can tell you what the underwater contour is like. The pond may be bowl shaped or fashioned like a frying pan. It could be a spring-fed body of water with drop-offs, humps, brush, timber, and everything else that makes for good bass fishing. As you begin to explore a pond, it makes sense to keep a notebook and make diagrams and notes wherever possible. If there is low water in midsummer, it can be worth a drive to look the pond over for map-making purposes. You'll be able to study a good part of the shoreline, and even some of the features in deeper water may stand out.

As a basic rule, a farm pond that offers a good deep-water structure usually does not produce an abundance of fish for anglers casting from the bank. It's the same as a big lake. If there is structure, shoreline fishing is never as good. On the other hand, if the pond doesn't have much structure in the middle, shoreline fishing should be much better, and you will achieve good results from the bank. Remember that a bass doesn't change its lifestyle just because it is in a farm pond. That lifestyle is tailored to the type of water and amount of cover.

FISHING FROM A BOAT

A farm pond or tiny lake is probably too small to allow you to fish from a standard bass boat with a high-horsepower outboard. Instead, you'll need a pram, canoe, johnboat, or even a rubber raft or belly boat. In many cases, a pair of oars or a paddle is all the propulsion you need; or you could use an electric motor.

If a permanently mounted depthsounder isn't feasible, there are several excellent portable models on the market that operate on batteries with transducers that clamp to the side of the boat. These depthsounders will read structure, and you can pinpoint any area with them.

Your first task is to learn the configuration of the pond and to locate structure. If the pond isn't too big, you can ease around in the boat, studying the shoreline and keeping an eye on the depthsounder. Try to orient the information the landowner gave you. If you see a creek enter the pond, trace its course. Use buoys to mark structure and then trace it out in your notebook so you have a rough map. Don't forget to name each spot so you can remember it.

If the farm pond is a large one, you might want to divide it into sections and explore each one independently, just as you would on a larger lake. Triangulation, of course, will assist you in returning to spots in the middle of the pond.

A farm pond is fished like any other bass water. You must strive to determine depth and then establish a pattern. The best places to find the correct depth are on sloping points into deeper water and along creek channels, just as in a large impoundment. The point to keep in mind is that the smaller pond is the same as a large lake, with the exception that there is less area to fish.

If you live and fish in the North, where farm ponds freeze over in winter, don't ignore the cold months for exploration. With ice covering the surface of the pond, you can walk over it and use a depth-sounder to map it out. When the ice melts in spring, the map you made in winter can prove invaluable.

A Typical Farm Pond

Illustration 47 depicts a typical farm pond with a considerable amount of structure. The waters you fish may have more or less structure, but let's use this as an example to discuss how we would fish this particular body of water. Note that this pond has a dam at one end; the water is usually deeper there. The corners of the dam (Positions 1 and 3) could be prime locations. The better corner would be the one that has more cover, has structure of some sort, and is closer to deeper water.

Position 2 marks the spot where the main creek channel is dammed off, and it could be excellent. Good fishing might be experienced in the channel near the dam, or you may have to work back up the channel until you find the pattern depth. Until you get to know the pond thoroughly, you may want to drop buoys over the creek channel and trace it out.

A point extends into the lake at Position 4, and since the water is usually deeper near the dam, you can assume that this will be a deep point. If the land falls off into a gradually tapering point, it would be an excellent spot to work for pattern depth. Check this area for brush piles, submerged stumps, and other features that could harbor bass.

At Position 5, a hump or high spot rises off the pond floor. Because of its proximity to the main creek channel, this location could hold plenty of fish. Keep in mind that bass may not always be over a particular type of structure, but they may use it from time to time. Therefore, it's always a good idea to keep going back to likely-looking areas, even if you only make a few casts.

The creek junctions at Positions 6 and 10 are worth fishing; depth will be the critical factor here, and the better junction will be the one with the proper pattern depth. At Position 7, there is a wide bend in the creek that is close to the creek junction and the high spot. The outside of this bend would be the better location, but you might want to try the inside as well. Again, buoys will help you to determine the layout of the creek channel.

A feeder creek enters the pond in a creek cove (Position 9), and this would be a great place during the spring, when largemouths

47. A typical farm pond

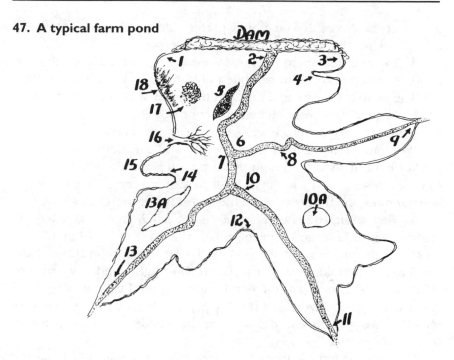

move into the shallows. If there were stickups, it might also be a prime spawning area. The creek then moves out into the pond to join the main channel. On the way, there is an S bend at Position 8. Note that this is the only sharp bend in the creek; the spot to fish is at the mouth of the bend.

A hole in the pond floor like the one at Position 10A can be productive. If you happen to be fishing a bowl-shaped pond without much in the way of structure, any hole or depression might hold a lot of fish. Unfortunately, in a bowl-shaped pond, holes or dents are tough to find, but once you uncover one, mark it well and keep checking it out.

Three creeks empty into our typical farm pond, and the one that starts at Position 11 is the largest. Experience tells us that, because it is the largest, it will probably hold more fish; this would indicate that it should be explored first.

You already know that a creek bed point is a choice spot, so Position 12 would be worth a maximum effort. It's an excellent feeding area, and if you work it enough times you should find fish there.

Another creek enters the pond at Position 13, and this situation is very similar to the one at Position 9. Look for stickups along the channel and check it out carefully in the spring, when fish could be back in the creek coves. If you find a pattern depth that works in one creek, look for the same depth in the other creeks.

A dip or depression in the pond floor (Position 13A) may not be as good as a deep hole, but it can often hold fish and is worth investigating. The same thinking carries over to the point at Position 14. It might not be as good as a creek channel point or one that extends into deep water, but if you're not catching fish at other spots, don't pass it up.

Position 15 marks a small pocket behind the point or an inside pocket cove. It's close enough to deep water and the creek channel to be interesting, and you might want to give it a try. Early morning or late afternoon might prove to be the better times to fish this cove.

Moving along the shoreline, we find a fallen tree at Position 16, standing or submerged objects out in the lake at Position 17, and grass, weeds, and moss at Position 18. These are all typical bass habitats. Objects should always be covered thoroughly, and any brush or submerged objects out in the pond require careful fishing. Weed beds can also be productive, and when oxygen levels are low you may very well find many of the fish right among the weeds, where oxygen content is maximized.

If a pond is fed by an underwater spring, keep in mind that the area around the spring will be cooler in summer and warmer in the cold months. It also produces oxygen-rich water, and fish will congregate around it whenever there is a question of sufficient oxygen.

WALKING THE BANKS

Many farm ponds either are too small to fish from a boat or don't have any feasible launching spots. In such cases your alternative is to walk the banks and cast. Before we even begin a discussion of bank fishing, one point must be emphasized. Anglers often forget that fish are particularly sensitive to sounds that are transmitted into the water, and that fish have the ability to see an angler standing on the bank. Like any other living creature, bass are aware of movement, and the motion of casting or your figure walking along the bank could chase fish into deeper water.

Just because everyone walks up to the water's edge doesn't mean that it is the correct way to fish. A better approach is a cautious one in which your clothing blends with the surroundings and you maintain a low profile. Instead of standing at the shoreline, force yourself to take up a position several feet back from the water's edge. By doing this, you won't spook as many fish, and your chances of catching bass increase manyfold. To convince yourself, look for bluegills along the shoreline in relatively shallow water. Then walk down toward them or wave your arm in the air so they can see the movement. If you are observant, you'll see the bluegills move away from the shoreline toward deeper water. Try another experiment. Stamp your feet along the bank and watch the bluegills. The sound should send them scurrying. Bass are no different, and if you practice a stealthy approach, it will result in a better catch.

If you are forced to walk the bank, you lose the advantage of a depthsounder, and you have no idea what lies below the surface of the water other than what the landowner told you. Of course, you still have your powers of observation, and you're going to put these to maximum use. The key will be irregular features or objects that are visible, plus a native knowledge of how creeks move, based on studying the shoreline.

When you walk the bank, it is important to fish each area thoroughly. The best way to do this is through a series of fan casts that systematically cover each sector of water. To establish a routine, you may want to fan in a clockwise direction. Start your first cast along the shoreline and then radiate each succeeding cast around the clock.

Just because you are fishing from shore doesn't mean that you can ignore pattern depth. It might be difficult to determine, but you should still attempt to work various depths. Let's say you are fishing a spinner. Make a cast and start the retrieve. Work through the entire circle of casts. Then start over again, but this time allow the lure to sink to a count of three or four before retrieving. Systematically cover the area. Then start a third time, letting the lure sink to a count of six or eight.

When you have fished various depths, move down the bank to the spot where your first cast hit the water and begin fan casting again. After you have covered 50 or 100 yards of shoreline without a strike, change lures and continue fishing the same pattern. Sometimes, direction of retrieve makes a difference. You may be casting into a cove without results. Move to the back end of the cove and cast again. The fish may prefer the lure moving from deep to shallow rather than the other way around. On another day, just the reverse might hold true, and you'll get your strikes as the lure travels from shallow to deep.

SEASONS

Farm-pond fishing is generally best in spring and fall, but it could continue throughout the year depending on where you live. In our judgment, a muddy farm pond in the winter would be difficult to fish; a *clear* pond in the winter would be a better bet, and it should be fished with light lines and small lures, even though it holds big bass.

As the water begins to warm in the spring, fish prefer fast-moving, vibrating lures. Of course, it depends on how muddy the pond is, but swimming baits are tough to beat during that time of the year. Good color combinations are yellow, black, iridescent colors, chartreuse, fluorescent red, and similar shades. Fish seem to detect and strike these colors better.

If you're walking the banks during the summer, switch to a lure such as a plastic worm or even a spinnerbait fished on the bottom. Swimming and vibrating baits may still be good if the pond remains muddy through the summer, or you may want to try a spinnerbait fished with a variety of retrieves. Don't forget to crawl the spinnerbait on the bottom, but in the very early morning or late afternoon, you may want to try some topwater baits.

As summer turns into fall, continue with the spinnerbait, fishing around objects and at different depths with various retrieves. Small spinners also produce fish, and don't discount the jig-and-eel.

In a clear farm pond during winter, you must fish slowly with small baits. A jig-and-eel or spinnerbait crawled along the bottom can work very well. Remember that the fish will move slowly and prefer very small baits, so rig and fish accordingly. You might also try small, flashy lures such as a Mepps spinner; or you could also use fall baits like the tail spins. If you can't locate fish at or near the bottom, then try a small swimming lure and fish various levels until you find the pattern depth.

If a pond is clear in the spring, it may pay to continue fishing the jig-and-eel on light lines. You can try a plastic worm, but in most places, bass ignore the worms until the water approaches 60° F. Flashy spinners might also produce fish, and if all else fails, try some small topwater baits fished parallel to the bank.

ANOTHER LOOK AT A TYPICAL FARM POND

Illustration 48 shows the same typical farm pond we fished from a boat earlier, but in this situation we will fish it from shore; the underwater features have been omitted.

We know that there should be deep water near the dam, so we'll start right there and try to determine the pattern depth through several series of fan casts fished at different depths. If we knew, from talking to the landowner, that one corner of the dam was better than the other because of some type of structure, we would start there.

On the first series of casts, the retrieve would be shallow. The second series would attempt a mid-depth retrieve, and the third

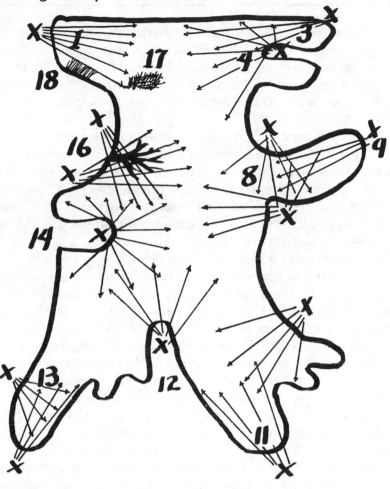

series of casts would probe the pond floor. It is important to establish a pattern depth as soon as possible. If the bass are holding at 3 feet, you want to know this; and you have to learn if they are at 12 feet or on the bottom.

Most lures will fall about 1 foot per second. Knowing this, you can use the countdown method to tell the depth at which your lure is traveling. From the instant the lure hits the water, start counting. Say to yourself, "One and two and three and four and five." Say it aloud at first, and there will be one second between each number, or 1 foot of depth. Count to five and the lure should be at 5 feet.

Whatever depth you catch your first fish is the depth you should continue fishing until you begin to suspect it might be wrong. Then go back to the countdown method and continue fishing until you hook another fish. That would be the new pattern depth, and you would fish it until you thought that conditions might have changed again.

The point at Position 4 would be fished with a series of fan casts, radiating from a cast parallel to the shoreline to systematic coverage of the deeper water. This is also a good spot to help determine pattern depth.

By looking back into the cove at Position 9, you should see the creek enter the pond. That tells you instantly that this is a creek cove, and you should realize that the creek channel is going to run through the cove and pass somewhere through the mouth of the cove. It may very well pass closer to one shore than the other, and this would be the better place. However, you may not be able to tell that at first, so you must fish both sides of the cove mouth carefully.

Then move back into the cove and fish the spot where the creek enters the pond. As you walk back toward the point where the creek enters the pond, fan a series of casts into the entire area. If that doesn't produce fish, stand at the back of the cove and cast out. Remember that sometimes the fish want the lure moving out of the cove, and at other times they want it moving back into the cove.

You should be able to assume (and then confirm by observation) that if the dam is at one end, the opposite end of the pond will be shallow. Position 11 delineates this type of shoreline, and it should be fished thoroughly with a series of fan casts from at least two or possibly three positions. Shallow ends are good places to fish during the spring and fall and on bright, sunny days in winter.

The point at Position 12 should be fished with fan casts covering the deeper water. Then move over to Position 13 and fish objects such as stumps, stickups, logs, and trees. You should be able to see a creek or ditch entering the pond at this spot. If not, cast the area from both sides anyway, but don't spend as much time as you would if there were a creek.

If there is a ditch or a creek, you will usually see stickups growing along the channel, and that's a prime way to confirm your suspicions. Don't forget to fish this cove from both sides and also from the tail end out into the deeper sections.

Positions 14, 16, and 18 should be fished with the same system of fan casts with which you handled other shoreline features. If you can see brush showing at Position 17 and can reach it with a cast, give it a try. Remember that you should be constantly experimenting with different lures, various colors, and as many variations in retrieve as you can come up with until you start catching fish.

Rivers and Creeks

FLOWING RIVERS CONNECT many impoundments and reservoir systems, and these rivers produce top-quality fishing. The one factor in river fishing that you don't have to contend with in lakes and ponds is the current; on rivers connecting a series of reservoirs, current speed can be governed by the amount of water released through a dam or spillway.

Before we get into a discussion of river fishing, we would be remiss if we did not direct your attention to the speed of river currents and the inherent dangers they can produce. Floating downstream in a boat, for example, you simply don't have very much control, and things can happen quickly. For that reason you must remain constantly alert to hazards of a navigational nature below you. It's easy to forget for an instant and suddenly look up to discover that your boat is being swept into a snag or a rock. An overhanging limb can knock an angler out of a boat and perhaps cause serious injury.

Life vests are a good investment, and we urge you to wear them when fishing rivers with fast currents. If you should happen to fall overboard, the life vest will help you to stay above water, and you'll need the added support to work toward shore with the current. The boat is going to be beyond your reach, so you can forget about it if you go overboard.

Above all, if you are fishing below a dam, stay alert to the discharge warnings and obey them. Discharges are usually signaled by a loud alarm system of a siren, bell, or combination. When you hear the warning, clear the area—regardless of how many strikes you are getting or how many bass you are adding to your stringer. Many dams produce a dangerous flow of water on a quick-discharge basis, causing extreme turbulence.

Remember also that the current is strongest near the dam and for a few miles below it. The farther below the dam you fish, the slower the current will be. Current is also dependent on whether the dam is discharging water or whether it has been several days since water flowed through the structure.

Fish have a tendency to move upstream and congregate around the base of a dam and for the first 3 or 4 miles downstream. One reason for this is that the flowing water sweeps plenty of food downstream from the reservoir above the dam, and it also catches food along the shoreline of the river and carries it downstream.

Whenever you fish in moving water such as a river with a current, there are two key points to keep firmly in mind. The first is that fish always face *into* the current. In a river, fish will be facing upstream unless they are alongside an eddy; in that case, they will be facing the direction of eddy flow. Second, it takes energy for a fish to maintain its lie in a moving current. Fish instinctively know that it is more efficient to minimize the energy expended, so they invariably take up positions where the main force of the current is interrupted by an object or by a depression in the bottom.

As a general rule, the current near the bottom is less than it is at the top of the water. If there is a depression, the fish can rest in this, and the main force of water will pass overhead. A boulder or a log with water bubbling around it creates a "hollow" or sheltered area where the current is minimal. There is usually "dead" water in front of and behind an obstruction, so the front and the back of a boulder, for example, would be worth exploring. Even though fish are out of the main current, they recognize that food will be swept along in the current, so they are almost always close enough to dart out, grab a morsel, and then ease back out of the current.

FISHING A FAST CURRENT

Water levels on rivers with a fast current fluctuate rapidly, and this affects both the fish and the fishing. The pattern is typical of flood-control systems and energy-creating systems such as the TVA. When water is pulled through the dam, the fish will begin to feed both in the lake above the dam and in the river below it. If the rise in river level is slow enough, fishing will be excellent, and you can find the fish moving into the newly flooded shallow areas along the shoreline.

The reason is that as the water level rises, food is washed into the river from the bank; bass are either waiting for that food or will move in to feed on smaller fish that in turn feed on insects and worms. On the other hand, a rapidly rising river often throws bass off their feed, and they will move out into deeper water until conditions settle down.

In most river systems, falling water is a signal to the fish to move off the banks and into deeper water. If the water level drops quickly, the fish have a tendency to move even deeper than normal until a stabilizing condition is reached. An exception to the rule takes place on the riverbed lakes of the Mississippi, where fish usually strike better on falling water. It's easy enough to learn the general pattern for any river system and, once you know the ground rules, simply follow them.

During the colder months, rivers are much better for smallmouths and Kentucky bass than they are for largemouths. For some reason, the largemouths become sluggish in cold rivers, but smallmouths remain vitalized by the extra oxygen that the current carries.

There are a number of choice locations in any river that should hold fish at one time or another. The area near a dam can be particularly productive. Mouths of feeder creeks or tributaries entering the main stream form junctions that hold fish (usually on the downcurrent side). If a feeder stream is belching muddy water into the primary flowage, look for fish along the edge of the off-colored water and not directly in it. They'll wait there, searching for food that gets swept out of the tributary and then pops into view in the cleaner water.

Any underwater obstruction will provide a resting station, because there is at least one eddy formed, and possibly more. Eddies in general are excellent places to find bass. They are off the main current, but the reverse flow of water will sweep food right past the fish and they don't have to work very hard to get it. Also, from an eddy a fish can move in and out of the current.

When the river makes a bend, it forms a bluff on one side and will shoal on the other. The down side of the shoal is a good place, and don't pass up the bluffs. As you work downstream and the current eases, these bluffs will have as many as five or six levels, and fish could be on any one of them.

Lures for River Fishing

The big problem in a river with any type of current is getting a bait down. Ordinarily, almost any bait that you can handle effectively in a lake will catch fish in a river, providing you can get the bait below the surface. Remember that, in a fast-moving stream, you may be drifting at from 3 to 8 miles per hour, depending on the current. That doesn't allow much time for the bait to sink to fish-eye level.

The best baits are those that will sink rapidly or perhaps dive down on the retrieve. One trick is to cast slightly upcurrent and allow the bait to sink a bit before retrieving, but you must develop a feel to do this effectively. Otherwise, the boat will be well downstream and you'll be dragging the lure behind the boat. The trick is to keep it near shore, where the fish are most likely to be.

We have found that in many rivers, fish hit a lure better when it is moving up against the current. Perhaps it is because the fish have a chance to see it and strike without exerting maximum energy, but it seems to work. If there is an eddy, let the eddy sweep the lure out of the current and back upstream. In an eddy, the lure should move with the current.

When you are fishing an obstruction such as a log, rock, or stump, cast so that the lure will pass alongside the obstacle and sweep along the narrowly defined edge of the main current or even lapse into the slower water. Fish hit a downstream-moving lure better under these conditions, or they will strike a lure that is cast into the obstruction and retrieved out. In general, however, we prefer right-angle casts and retrieves or those that move the lure slightly upstream, except for the situations we have noted.

RIVER HOT SPOTS

Each river is going to have its own course, contour, and configuration, but there are many features that are common to the majority of rivers you will fish. Let us point out that it is also possible to fish structure in a river wherever you find it, and a depthsounder can be a valuable aid in your search for productive spots. A submerged brush pile or rock bed can produce plenty of fish. Always watch the shoreline carefully; changes in soil content from mud to gravel to clay to sand can be indicative of holding areas for fish. Frequently, bass take up stations along a transitional zone, so stay alert to any changes in terrain.

Study illustration 49, which depicts an S bend in a river. Bluffs form on the bank that the current strikes, while there is a shoal area opposite the bluff. The beginning of the bluff could be a good spot, and it pays to look along the bluff for any objects, such as fallen timber or stumps, that could hold fish. The better place to fish, however, would be on the downcurrent edge of the shoal on the other side of the river.

If you're looking for a reason, the current is seldom as strong on the back end of the shoal as it is on the forward portion; and the water often tapers off on the back side, dropping into deeper water.

49. River bends

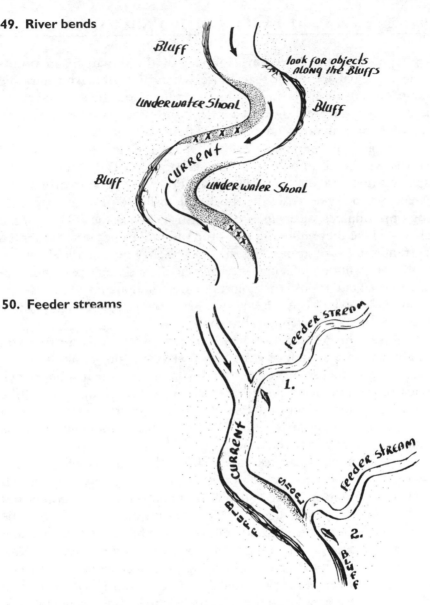

50. Feeder streams

On rivers where the current isn't very strong, fish may move over the entire shoal area, so it is important to cast the shoals carefully.

Wherever a feeder stream enters the main current is an excellent place to fish (illustration 50). You'll find that the downcurrent point is usually better than the opposite point. One reason is that a waiting predator can take advantage of any forage fish washed down from the feeder stream. When bait is picked up by the main river current, it is swept right past the downcurrent corner.

Note in this illustration that a second stream enters the main river right below a shoal. We have found that the downcurrent points below a shoal are better than those where the tributary enters the main current directly. There is less current under these conditions, and the fish can roam the area a little more, rather than being "pinned down" behind an obstruction to avoid fighting the current.

An island in the middle of the river will divert the current, and shoals will build up on either side (illustration 51). If you study the split current carefully, you will usually find that the current is much weaker on one side. That's the shoal, which should provide better fishing opportunities. Again, most of the fish will be at the tail end of the shoals where they either slope or drop off into deeper water, but if the current is not very strong, the fish could be anywhere on the shoal.

There will be bluffs opposite the shoals, and don't pass these up without taking a look. Any objects or obstructions on the bluffs are worth fishing; look specifically for a stair-step effect of ledges where the current is not exceptionally strong.

Illustration 52 demonstrates other types of structure that you might find in a stretch of river. The first thing you should notice is that most of the fish will be on the downcurrent side of stumps, rock piles, or even points. A point, for example, will break the force of the current and turn it outward. Fish can lie in comfort behind the point and dart out to grab passing food or wait until a minnow works its way into the calmer waters.

Dips or pockets can also hold fish for the same reasons. The current, of course, sweeps by but doesn't always swing into the pocket. If you see a stump row, the fish will be behind the obstructions, but don't forget to consider the sun. Make your maximum effort when the shady side is downcurrent. Rock piles can also be very productive, and the exact location of the fish depends on many factors. Think in terms of current and try to figure out how high the pile extends off the bottom and the effect it has on water flow. If the water is bubbling, there should be a lee area in front of the rocks and another at the tail. The tail would usually be the better choice, but a few well-placed casts that sweep by the head of the pile can bring strikes.

If the rocks are large, fish might be anywhere along the length of the pile, seeking cover behind a specific boulder but in position to grab passing food. Remember that your quarry seeks shelter from the current, but maintains a position where it can feed easily.

We mentioned a moment ago that you should always keep sun direction in the back of your mind as you scout a river for fishy-looking spots. Illustration 53 demonstrates that the shady banks are fre-

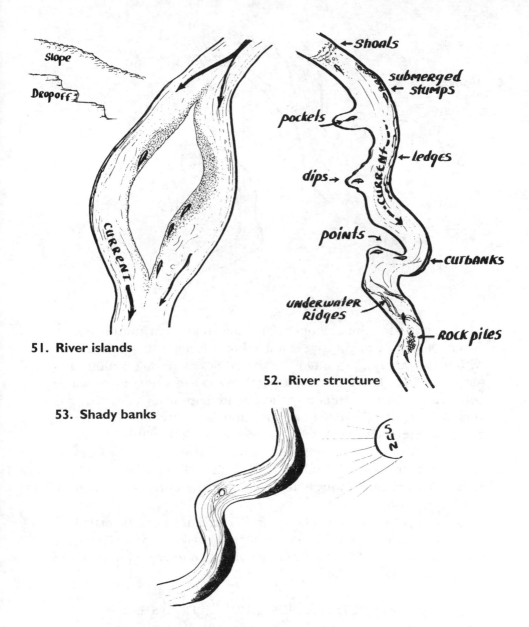

51. River islands

52. River structure

53. Shady banks

quently better. When you find other conditions being met, consider the sun. If the bank you are fishing is in shade and there is a shoal tapering off, a point, a dip, a pocket, or obstructions, the chances of fish being present are increased. We are not saying that you can't catch fish on the sunny side, but a good spot is even better when it lies in the shade. Sometimes you may decide to come back to a particular area late in the day when the sun will not hit it, or perhaps fish it first thing in the morning before the sun clears the treetops. These might seem like subtle points, but they can be extremely important.

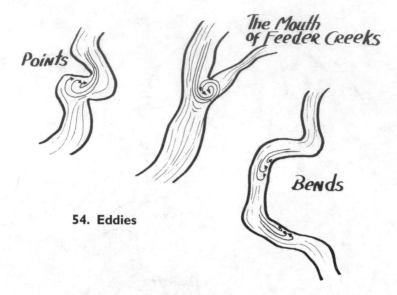

54. Eddies

There is something about eddies that tells even the beginning fisherman that he might have stumbled on a feeding station. In a river with a fast current, fish often use the eddies as resting stations and places to feed. There is even a narrow zone of transitional water between the main current and the countercurrent or eddy that has very little water movement. Illustration 54 shows three types of places where eddies are likely to occur. An eddy could be set up as water swirls around a point extending into the river. Look for foam on the surface or leaves and other debris that collect in one spot. Any gathering of floating objects tells you that the current is relatively dead in that spot.

An eddy can also form where a feeder stream enters the main current, and you can find eddies where the river makes a bend. The point is to be alert to the formation of them and then to capitalize on them by fishing the area carefully.

SMALLMOUTHS IN NORTHERN RIVER SYSTEMS

Throughout the Northeast and Middle Atlantic states, a number of rivers offer prime smallmouth habitat. The upper reaches of the Susquehanna, Potomac, Shenandoah, Delaware, and James Rivers are smallmouth strongholds, and there are many other streams in New York, Pennsylvania, Maryland, Virginia, and West Virginia that produce their share of this great gamefish.

All these rivers have a current flow of 1 to 4 knots, but even though smallmouths prefer fast-moving water, they remain out of the main current. Most of these rivers are rocky, and unless a smallmouth moves out to pick off a passing morsel, you'll find the fish stationed behind rocks that break the current.

Learning to read the water is the secret of successfully fishing these rivers. Watch the shoreline and the way the rocks enter the water. Most people think you only fish the downstream side of the rocks, but it depends on how the rock is positioned in the water. If the rock slants sharply into the water on the upstream side, but drops off on the back side, then the place to cast is the back portion of the rock. A rock that is almost vertical in front will pile the water up, creating a dead spot in *front* of the rock, and smallmouths will take advantage of it.

Another trick is to watch foam lines or drift lines of dead leaves. This will tell you how the current is swinging. The Native Americans and early settlers often built funnels to help them net fish (called fish pots), and although they were destroyed by law back around the turn of the century, you can often see the remains. Sometimes there is enough left to channel the water to some extent, and there will be a slick glide in the fast-moving water in front of them. The same holds true with low dams.

These slick glides can be a haven for large smallmouths, because the fish are there looking for food and very few anglers fish these places. Look for them. When you find a low dam, the water will be bubbling and boiling over the top, but 2 to 3 feet below, there is virtually no current. Here the smallmouths can hold in comfort, rising quickly to take a bait and dropping right back down.

The way to fish these low dams is with surface lures. Cast downstream where the water breaks over the dam and use your rod tip to work the plug back upstream with painstaking slowness. You want to simulate a small fish that is fighting desperately to keep from being swept over the dam. If there is a smallmouth in front of the dam, chances are it will rise and grab the plug.

From early May through June, many of these rivers will give birth to willow grass beds with stems that are only 3 to 4 inches high. Three- and 4-pound smallmouths (which are trophy fish for that part of the country) move over these grass beds in search of minnows, and you can do well with a small plug retrieved quickly.

When you cast a plug on a river, the current instantly starts to sweep it downstream. If you imparted only occasional action, the lure would be passing over stretches of water in a lifeless state. To catch fish, the lure should be moving most of the time in a twitch-stop-twitch-stop-twitch-stop rhythm.

Over the grass beds, plastic worms rigged on a size 1 hook can be extremely effective. Cast the worm upstream, let it sink to the bottom and tumble over the grass beds. Six-inch worms are about the maximum length, and they should be fished on light spinning gear. As the worm tumbles downstream, keep the bail on your reel open, closing it only long enough to take the slack out of the line. When you feel a strike, let the fish run 8 or 10 feet before setting the hook. Otherwise, you'll miss more fish than you hook.

Underwater lures are great smallmouth catchers, and those with short stroke and vibration seem to do best. In fast water, a smallmouth can see an underwater lure better. Spinners can really do a job, and there's a special way to fish them. Most anglers insist on casting across the stream and then retrieving as the lure swings below them. A spinner is intended to represent the motion and flash of a baitfish. The most effective flash comes when the blade is rotating at the slowest possible speed. We already know that smallmouths live near the bottom, so the trick is to combine maximum flash with a lure that scratches along just above the rocks. Instead of casting across and letting the lure swing downstream, make your cast across the stream, but *upstream*. Let the lure sink for a moment and then retrieve as slowly as you can, perhaps one or two revolutions ahead of a tight line. This will cause the lure blade to turn slowly, because instead of fighting the current, the blade is going with the current.

A little practice will give you the necessary feel to keep the lure just above the rocks without letting it snag. You can also adjust the depth of the lure by either raising or lowering your rod tip. If the spinner hangs, vibrate the rod in short, sharp side motions and it will usually knock the spinner loose.

MORE SMALLMOUTH TIPS

If you use a minnow-type lure, cast it out and twitch it back to you on the surface. Don't swim it under water. The fish will come topside to hit it, and you'll find that by sliding it across the surface, you get more strikes.

Studies have been made that prove that smallmouths do not move around a great deal during their lifetime. If you locate a big bass near a ledge, chances are it won't range more than a quarter mile. When you do catch a big bass, continue to work the area for another 10 or 15 minutes. There could be more fish in the same area; and check back in a day or two, because another one will move in. Big bass dominate choice locations, and if the spot suited one husky critter, you can bet it would make a good home for another.

In the spring, quite a few smallmouths will concentrate below the bases of dams. We're not certain whether they do this because there is more oxygen, because they are anticipating an impending migration to spawn, or for some other reason, but they are there and that's the place to fish for them.

Most people don't use surface lures for smallmouth fishing during summer on these rivers, but if you're willing to fish after dark, you can limit out on topwater baits. The better fishing is not early in the morning as you might suspect, but late in the afternoon, continuing into the night. Although it has been around a long time, the Jitterbug makes one of the best nighttime smallmouth lures, because it produces a constant vibration on the surface of the water.

Speaking of night smallmouth fishing on Northeast rivers, prime territory is over the grass beds where the bigger fish move in to feed under the cover of darkness. They will also hang out in front of a low dam, but you won't find many fish after dark in the middle or along the tail of a dam.

Besides the major rivers, there are many smaller streams averaging 25 to 40 feet in width that offer superb smallmouth fishing. Many of these are the lower ends of trout streams, where the water is a little too warm to support a trout population but is perfect for smallmouths. In many places, these streams are too shallow to float a boat, yet they are ideal for wading.

In a small stream, you should always wade upstream. If you wade downstream, debris and mud that you kick up with your feet will move downstream ahead of you, serving to constantly put the fish on the alert. Also, since fish face the current, you can attain a better approach if you move up from behind than you possibly could by wading right down on the fish.

For top-quality sport, try an ultralight spinning outfit about 5½ feet long with mono line in the 2- to 4-pound-test range. One of the best lures you can select is a small, floating Rapala type that will dive when it is retrieved. By casting upstream, you can work a pool thoroughly by first twitching the lure and then causing it to dive and pop back to the surface. The tail end of the pool should be shallow, so you can float the plug over this section with a series of twitches that cause the nose to dive and pop back up. Very often, a smallmouth will hit it before it leaves the pool.

Weather, Water, and Seasons

ABOUT THE TIME you think you have carefully considered all the factors that motivate the behavior of bass and have cataloged them into a precise sequence, your quarry is going to begin playing the game with a whole new set of rules. Bass fishing is like that, and that is what makes it so great.

All of us know that weather affects fish behavior, and that this behavior can be amplified by the season of the year and the type of water. The problem is that fish aren't always affected the same way. And we might as well tell you that there are no rigid rules. Certain lakes, for example, have their own peculiarities, while latitude will introduce another variable.

The key to capitalizing on the changes in weather, water, and seasons is a degree of alertness on your part and the willingness to continue to observe and record your findings in the lakes that you fish most often. Very frequently, bass on another lake will react the same way to atmospheric changes, and your experiences in one area will pay dividends in another.

Recognize that there are differences between muddy, dingy, and clear water. The windy side of a lake might not be the same as the lee shore; a high barometer has a different effect on bass than a fast-falling barometer; cloudy days can cause bass to modify their behavior pattern from what it was on a sunny day. Fish may not be in the same "lunker holes" in spring, even though you found them there last fall. These examples serve to illustrate the complexity of the problem and the infinite number of variables that guard the solution to where a bass will be and when. We'll give you some of our general observations as a starting point, and we hope you'll pursue the subject on your own favorite bass waters.

WEATHER AND WATER

During a fishing tournament, we had a school of bass pinpointed in 15 feet of water. The sun was shining, and we'd hook a bass with every third or fourth cast using a blue plastic worm. Suddenly, the activity stopped. Our first reaction was to analyze what we were doing and what could have happened. Before we got halfway through this approach, we began to catch fish again. Then the fish stopped a second time.

Searching for an answer, we noticed that the sky had begun to cloud over with big, puffy, white clouds. Taking this one step farther, we then discovered that when the sun was covered by a cloud, the fish stopped hitting. In clear water on bright days, blue worms have been a favorite of ours, but on cloudy days we prefer black. So without hesitating, we switched to a black worm and started to catch fish when the sun was blotted out. As soon as the cloud passed, the black worm became a futile effort, so we switched back to blue.

To satisfy our own curiosity (and we're sure yours, too), we then rigged two rods—one with a blue worm and the other with a black one—and conducted an experiment. As unbelievable as it might sound, when the sun was out, we could cast a black worm and never get a hit. Toss the blue worm in the same spot and a bass would take it. The reverse held true when the sun wasn't shining.

You might think that this is an isolated instance, and it well might be, but it does point up the importance of being observant and of modifying your techniques to gain harmony with the weather. As a general rule, most bass fishermen prefer overcast days to those when the sun is shining brightly. For one thing, the fish might be a little shallower when the sun isn't out, and for another, they are easier to approach. We believe fish are more active on cloudy days, yet the best time to fish is when you are there, and that includes sunny days.

On a bright day in a clear lake, our preference would be for dingy water rather than the windowpane-clear water, and we'll take the time to search for colored water. That doesn't mean that the water will be muddy, but it will be somewhere in the transitional zone where fish will respond better.

Of course, we have continually pointed out that bass are sensitive to bright light; on a sunny day, the odds are in your favor if you concentrate your fishing on the shady side of an obstacle or along a shady bank. If you are fishing a creek channel, work the submerged bank that is on the shady side.

The barometer must also be considered seriously. If we were given a choice, a slowly rising barometer seems to provide the best fishing for us; and we have done well on a fast-falling barometer at times. That follows the theory that fish bite well just before a storm. On the other hand, an extremely high barometer has produced poor fishing for us more times than not, and a slowly falling glass also creates problems. This doesn't mean that you can't catch fish under those conditions, but they just don't seem to be as good as other times.

Let's delve into water clarity once more so that you'll have it firmly implanted in your mind. The rule is that the muddier the water, the shallower the fish will be. In a very muddy lake, you probably won't find bass deeper than perhaps 15 feet. At the same time, you must tailor your selection of lure colors to those that will be visible, and that's the place to concentrate on vibrating baits. In a clear lake, you'll do better with lighter lines and smaller lures, and the fish will be relatively deeper than they would be in dingy or muddy water.

Although wind can be enough of a nuisance to make fishing uncomfortable, it can also be an ally and help you find fish. The windy side of a lake is often better because the breeze creates more oxygen, and it also pushes baitfish against that shore. The ripple it creates also gives bass a slightly stronger sense of security, and they may be a bit shallower than they would be if the lake were slick calm; and wind masks the surface of the water, permitting you to approach closer to your target without being detected. This is always important, but even more so in a clear lake where you can consider wind to create additional cover.

Fishing is often better along the ripraps that border a dam when they are on the windy shore; the same seems to hold true with bluff walls. If the wind isn't too strong, our preference is to concentrate on the windy side of the lake, but if the zephyrs approach a tropical disturbance, we'll seek the shelter of the lee shoreline.

You already know that oxygen is much more important to a fish than temperature and the natural comfort zone of 68° to 72° F. Wind adds oxygen to the water, and on very hot days during the summer, when water temperatures are above the 80° F mark, you'll often find bass in shallow water on the windy side, trying to glean the extra oxygen.

Speaking of water temperatures, we should make it clear that the comfort zone is merely a guideline, and that bass will leave their preferred temperature range for a variety of reasons. However, to find a pattern it is necessary to have a starting point, and the comfort zone provides a place to begin. Experience and judgment (plus a gut feeling, at times) will help you to modify your thinking and probe outside the comfort zone when conditions warrant.

If you are fishing a lake in the middle of summer or winter, when oxygen levels in the lake would normally be low, do most of your fishing around milfoil, if it's present. Bass will swarm around it because of the oxygen it produces. Many a veteran fisherman will tell you to look for coontail moss during periods of low oxygen; when you find it, you'll find the bass.

WINTER FISHING

It wasn't too many years ago that most bass fishermen would pull their boats out of the water and hang up their tackle for another season just about the time that the weather was getting chilly. In fact, there are still some northern states with bass seasons that legally end in the fall and don't open again until late spring or early summer. However, in other northern waters, bass are taken through the ice during the middle of winter, and anglers across the nation are beginning to recognize the potential of winter bass fishing.

Latitude plays an important part in winter fishing. For purposes of our discussion, we will eliminate those waters that lie far enough south so that the water temperatures never really drop far below the comfort zone of the bass; instead, our thoughts will center on those areas where water temperatures might drop into the 50s and might even get down to 40° F.

A number of bass fishermen erroneously believe that bass disappear during winter, but obviously this is not true. Since all fish are cold-blooded creatures, their metabolic rates are directly affected by surrounding water temperatures. Body functions are at the norm when bass reside within their comfort zone, but as water temperatures fall, the fish become sluggish. They don't need as much food to sustain themselves, and their digestive rates are correspondingly slower.

Significantly, bass will not chase a lure very far in cold water, and they are more prone to pick up smaller tidbits than to attempt to gorge themselves on larger prey. A fisherman's understanding of this is the key to winter fishing in many areas of the country. When you are fishing cold water, *think slow*. The idea is to fish a lure as slowly as you can, and even then, you're still probably fishing it too fast. Old Mr.

Largemouth isn't about to work for food, and a bass that is ravenous in the summer can probably, in 40° F water, get by on about one-tenth its usual food intake.

To be successful when water temperatures are low, you must either drop a falling lure right in front of a bass or inch a lure along the bottom so that it tantalizingly passes directly in front of your quarry. If you insist on buzzing a spinnerbait in cold water, your chances of success are virtually nil.

During the winter bass often school, and schooling usually takes place according to the size of the fish. Fish in the 1- to 3-pound class will be together, and larger fish, in the 4- to 8-pound range, will school separately; they can really bunch up tightly, with an armada of fish taking up little room in the water. On new lakes, schooling by size doesn't always hold true, although we can't tell you why. However, on a young lake you may find 2-pounders mixed in with 6-pounders.

Depth is also a problem in the winter. Fish can be anywhere from 2 to 70 feet or deeper; it all depends on the weather and the specific lake. Normally, however, fish will be deeper in the winter; and they will be deeper in a highland lake than they will be in a midland or lowland lake. The deeper they go, the more difficult they are to locate and catch. It is certainly tough to fish a light lure very deep and still maintain the necessary control and feel.

Although bass do go deeper in highland lakes, they'll move up closer to the surface on calm, bright days in the winter. They'll still be over deeper water rather than the shallows, but they'll suspend in the tops of submerged trees, or you'll find them in the flooded timber areas. Our fishing preference during the cold weather is a midland lake such as Tennessee's Pickwick. The waters are clear, with rock bluffs and gravel bars, and the fish don't seem to stay as deep in this type of lake.

Regardless of the type of tackle you prefer during the rest of the year, winter fishing dictates ultralight spinning gear with lines testing 4, 6, and sometimes 8 pounds. Obviously, if you are fishing lowland lakes such as Toledo Bend or Sam Rayburn, you'll need heavier lines in the timber areas, but the light mono works well for schooling fish over open water.

Spinning has many advantages at this time of year. It allows you to cast the very light lures that are necessary, and there is more "give" to spinning than bait casting, so you won't break a light line as easily. Our choice is a rather stiff rod that measures 5 or 5½ feet in length.

Not only does this type of rod have plenty of backbone to handle bigger fish, but the stiff tip is much more sensitive than a soft one, and it allows you to feel the lure.

There's no question that you'll get more hits on light lines and small lures. Among the better winter baits are structure spoons, jig-and-eels, jigs, single spins, and twin spins. Jigs should be ⅛ or ¼ ounce at the most, made of bucktail, polar bear hair, or marabou with a 4-inch split-tail eel trailing from the hook. The best colors are a white jig with a white tail, yellow jig with a yellow tail or a white tail, black jig with a black tail, brown with a black tail, or yellow with a black tail. Take your pick, but our favorites are a white jig with white tail or a yellow jig with a white tail. These same color combinations work well on smallmouths and Kentuckys.

Cast the lure into a bluff, along a point, over a drop-off, around an object, or wherever there is structure. As the lure hits the water, close your bail and take up the slack line. Remember that you must fish the lure as a fall bait, and that bass will frequently hit it on the way down. If you can keep the boat in one position during the cast, it's easier to feel the lure.

Again, you must walk a tightrope, allowing the lure to fall freely, but keeping the line tight so you can feel a fish take it. This is important. Watch the line closely, because you will usually *see* the strike (a slight pull on the line) before you feel it. You must try to fish the bait as smoothly as possible, and this, of course, depends on how deep you must probe. Hold the rod tip steady slightly above a 45-degree angle and really concentrate on what you are doing.

Sometimes we'll twitch the wrist slightly, giving the bait a little action. At other times we'll let it fall, twitch or swim it just a hair, and then let it fall again. If the lure hits a ledge, ease it off and let it fall again. If you keep score, you'll discover that 99.9 percent of the time the bass will hit the lure on the fall. The less you do to the lure and the less action you impart, the more fish you will catch. Keep the rod and line as motionless as possible and watch for the unmistakable "flick" in the line when a bass picks it up.

Bass anglers sometimes look down on those who use spinning tackle, but in the winter, light spinning is the best method on midland and highland lakes. The terrain might be rugged and you may have to go a little heavier, but when you can get away with 4- or 6-pound-test line, use it. It will produce a lot more fish than winch outfits with 20-pound-test, and you'll have more fun in the process.

NIGHT FISHING

If you are fishing a relatively clear lake during late spring, summer, or early fall, and if you're not catching fish during the day, try the lake at night. Big bass are sometimes deep and tough to locate during daylight hours. At night the lake comes alive, and these same fish may move into 3 to 10 feet of water to feed. Darkness gives them cover, and it also makes it easier for them to expend less energy in attacking their prey.

The strange world of night fishing is a thrill that most fishermen never know. Beautiful scenery is replaced by solitude, night sounds are amplified, and this is the time when a sensitive rod tip and a good pair of hands make all the difference. Nights are peaceful on the water, and the hustle and bustle of boats, water-skiers, and swimmers is replaced with the haunting sounds of hoot owls and feeding fish.

There is little doubt that on very clear lakes you'll catch more fish at night and bigger fish than at any other time. Night fishing begins to get good when the water temperature rises into the upper 50s, but it is best when the thermometer reads well above 60° F. Any lake that contains a healthy population of crawfish or spring lizards (salamanders) is usually a good night lake. If the lake is rocky or has gravel, these are the areas that would hold crawfish and are therefore prime bass locations. Crawfish move around a lot more at night than they do in the daytime, especially after a rain or when the wind is blowing against the bank. Off-colored water on the windward side is excellent, and you'll also do well where there is a drain or runoff; and don't pass up mud or gravel banks with deep water nearby.

The jig-and-eel and the spinnerbait are good night lures on most lakes during the spring and fall of the year. During the summer, a plastic worm or a spinnerbait will take more fish. Crawl these baits right along the bottom, because bass will be searching the lake floor for crawfish or salamanders. At night on a lowland or midland lake that does not stratify, bass will often move into 3, 4, or 5 feet of water to feed. Lakes that do stratify through the summer—mountain or highland lakes—are also good at night, but the fish will feed deeper than they will in lowland or midland lakes. Surface plugs also often provide exciting action at night.

If you are going to fish a lake at night, it's important to know it well so that you can locate bass hangouts—and also for safety reasons. The best procedure is to study the lake for a day or two during the daytime to learn your way around and to know where dangerous navigational obstacles lie. A lake with a lot of trees and stumps can be tricky at night; as you scout it in the daytime, select those routes from spot to spot that will be easiest to travel at night.

Since there won't be many fishermen on a lake after dark, you must be even more safety conscious than you are in the daytime, and prepare for any emergency. Besides extra spark plugs for your motor and a full complement of spare parts, your boat should be rigged with navigational lights, and you should carry emergency-type lights and flares. Water-safety devices and life jackets are a must.

In our experience, it doesn't really make a difference whether you fish on a bright night or on one when the moon isn't shining. Bass seem to feed as well on a moonlit night as they do during the new moon. However, you can certainly see better when the moon is out, and navigation is a little easier then. If the moon is bright, treat it just as you would the sun and concentrate your fishing on the shady side of objects or along a shady shoreline.

Once your eyes become oriented to the darkness, make certain that you don't look at bright lights or even a cigarette lighter. This will temporarily destroy your night vision and it could be several minutes before it returns. Fish are also sensitive to light at night, because their eyes are geared to darkness. If you shine a light across the water, and especially along the area you want to fish, you'll probably succeed in chasing every bass out of the area. Scientists call it light shock; the fish panics when suddenly confronted by bright light. It's similar to the way you feel when you walk out of a dark theater into bright sunlight.

In planning a night trip, you should concentrate on organizing your tackle and your boat so that you can find anything easily and without the use of lights. If you own a number of outfits, rig up four to six of them with various lures you might want to try. That way, you can change lures by merely picking up another rod; you won't have to use a light to tie on a new bait. At the same time, your tacklebox should be arranged so that you can get to anything blindfolded (or in the dark). This little bit of preparation can make night fishing much easier and more enjoyable.

Finally, you should understand a little bit about the moon. On the night of a full moon, the moon will rise exactly at sunset and stay visible in the sky throughout the day and the night. In the middle latitudes, on the day after the full moon, the moon will rise about 40 minutes after sunset. The second night after the full moon, moonrise will be 1 hour and 20 minutes after sunset. Each night, the moon rises approximately 40 minutes later and it gets smaller in size until there is no moon at all.

At new moon, you won't see any moon at all. The next night there will be a tiny sliver of moon at sunset, and it will stay up for about 40 minutes; on each succeeding night, the moon will stay up 40 minutes longer, until full moon.

SPRING AND SPAWNING

The coming of spring not only pumps adrenaline through the veins of every bass master, but their quarry also becomes more active. Warming waters send bass into the shallows to feed and to spawn, making it the perfect time of year for fast fishing action.

Perhaps the most important piece of equipment you can own in the springtime is a temperature gauge. Things happen fast as the sun moves north of the equator; temperature is the tip-off. For one thing, shallow water warms faster than the deeper portions of a lake, and bass will prowl the shallows to feed. Way back in creek coves is a perfect spot to look for bass, especially if there are plenty of stickups along the channel. Keep in mind that bass are cold-blooded and, as the water warms, their metabolism quickens its pace. Digestion rates increase, and the need for more food correspondingly rises. There will be more food in the shallows at that time of year, so that's where your quarry is going to be.

In some lakes, the transition can be so sudden that fishermen are often taken by surprise. One or two warm rains after a rugged winter can bring fish up overnight, and they'll herd into the shallows like charging rhinos.

Determining spawning time is not difficult as long as you are willing to take water temperatures. About the time that the thermometer reads in the high 50s or low 60s (this, of course, depends on the latitude), bass will be over the nests. Largemouths spawn in relatively shallow water, smallmouths just a bit deeper. How shallow they are depends on the clarity of the lake and the amount of cover. In a clear lake without much cover, spawning will take place deeper than it would in a dingy lake with plenty of places to hide.

For best results, working the shallows requires a stealthy approach. When bass are over a nest, you can flush them and they'll return, but it is far better to approach silently and make a good presentation the first time. Since water temperatures are on the rise and fish are more active, you can move the bait much faster than you normally would in cold water.

Throughout most of the South, plastic-worm fishing doesn't really prove effective until after the water temperature reaches 60° F, but in some northern areas, worms have taken bass when temperatures were below 50° F. Spinnerbaits are a good choice over the beds and whenever bass move into the shallows.

FALL FRENZY

Some say it's the shorter photo period (length of daylight), others point out that the sun has moved south and the rays are no longer directly overhead, even at noon, while still others tell you it's the dropping water temperatures. Whatever the reason, bass seem to move into the shallows for one last feeding binge before winter grips the landscape; it is a great time for capitalizing on largemouth movements.

Bass will occupy a variety of habitats during the tail end of the year, but one excellent place to look is in coves, especially those with creeks emptying into them. Cooler temperatures allow the fish to be comfortable in shallow water, and they know they have to take on plenty of food to add weight before their metabolism slows.

The exact dates, of course, depend on latitude, and things are going to happen earlier in the North than they will in the South, but that's merely timing. In lakes with large populations of shad, the bait will be tightly schooled and bass will be lurking nearby, often feeding on the surface.

You'll find jig-and-eel combinations along with spinnerbaits and tail spins to be good lures for this time of year, and you can also do well on topwaters. The point to remember is that your quarry is going to be on the move; your first task is to locate the fish. Be particularly alert to changing water temperature during this period and, as the mercury plummets (in the water), begin to switch to smaller baits and slower retrieves.

Just like spring, fall is a transitional period, and you must constantly modify your techniques to take maximum advantage of the weather. There will be warm, bluebird days, and there will be times when cold fronts plunge through the region. Cold fronts, by the way, often produce excellent fishing, and you might find that largemouths go on a feeding spree just before a front passes through. They instinctively know that the weather is going to be bad for a few days.

So while other anglers have already quit for the year and turned to watching football on TV, if your state permits bass fishing through November or year-round, you could capitalize on the fall frenzy that takes place every year.

Index

afternoon fishing, 2, 48, 88, 90, 99, 103
alertness, 15, 21, 77, 80, 93, 104
approach, 19, 70, 71, 76, 79-80, 88-89
area selection, 75-76
artificials, 6, 81, 90, 105, 113

bait, 72, 80, 81, 96, 110; fall, 67, 90, 109; school of, 6, 113; swimming, 53, 66, 90; topwater, 66, 68, 72-73, 90, 103; vibrating, 90, 106; winter, 90, 109
bait casting. *See* casting
baitfish, 6, 36, 37, 63, 65, 106
bank: reading the, 56-57; walking the, 88-89
bank fishing, 56-57, 88-92, *91*
banks, shady, 98, *99*
barometer, effects of, on bass, 106
bass: lifestyle of, 7-8, 85; suspended, 52-55, *54*, 61, 108
Bass Anglers Sportsman Society (BASS), 11
bass water, 3-4, 11, 105-107
belly boats, 85
bends: creek, 30, 31, 35, 86, 87; ox box, 43; river, 95, 96, *97*, 100; s, 43, *44*, 96; u, 43, *44*, 47, 48, 76
Bennett, Dr. George, 9
black bass characteristics, 1-3
blowdown, *69*
bluegills, 9, 88, 89
bluff bank, 38, 59, *60*
bluff channel, *60*

bluffs: creek, 38-41, *40, 43*, 45; fishing, 59-62; paralleling, *62;* river, 95, 98
boats, 19, 75; on ponds, 85-86
bottom, 7, 16, 18, 24, 57-58, 78. *See also* structure
bridges, submerged, 50, *51*
bucktails, 81, 82, 83, 109
Bull Shoals Lake, 22
bunching, 39, 53
buoys. *See* marker buoys
buzzing, 66, 73, 108

canoe, 85
casting, 18, 19, 66, 67, 79-80, 81, 96, 101, 102, 103, 109; accuracy of, 12-13
casts, fanning, 13, 18, 19, 53, 61, 68, 69, 79, 89, 90, 92
charts, 74-75
clothing, anglers', 88
cloudy days, 63, 80, 104, 105. *See also* weather
cold fronts, 113-14
color: bait, 82, 105, 106; lure, 3, 72, 82, 90, 92; spoon, 72
color perception, bass, 3, 90, 105, 106
comfort zone, 18, 106, 107. *See also* temperature, water
compass sighting, 25
competition, 10-11
confidence, 11-14
Corps of Engineers, U.S., 23, 75
countdown method, 19-21, 53, 55, 91, 92

115